WHAT OTHERS ARE SAYING ABOUT BLUE STILEY AND
THE SUM OF 4

"Blue Stiley shares many lessons learned in his formative years that are critical to effective leadership throughout life. I found myself smiling as I related to a great number of things in these pages that I see in my leadership style, while wincing at other things I know I need to improve. I like how Blue crystalizes/exhibits good leadership skills on a very personal level with the mentor/mentee relationship, which I found very easy to relate to and extremely valuable. I definitely took away some very clear to dos to work on with my own mentoring skills."

— Robert Dodson
CEO, Ricardo Beverly Hills Inc.

"Navigating today's world is a lot different than it once was. We have access to everyone without whole truths. We don't know how people got to where they are or if they're even happy, but we see pictures and believe we're less than them. Why? Blue Stiley is a real person speaking real truths on how to look in the mirror, instead of Instagram, and be truly inspired by what we see—not only by telling us how to do it, but by showing us how through real-life experiences. Blue's discipline and positivity is second to none. He is a voice here to serve and inspire. If you need a push or a little direction, you've come to the right place."

— Nina Hajian
Morning Show Host Entercom Radio

"Thought-provoking and inspiring, all while being incredibly relatable! *The Sum of 4* is a great read for anyone looking to forge a new path, and not only improve themselves, but help others grow along the way—just like Blue has done for all of his students and clients."

— Kaitlin Hawayek
Team USA Figure Skater

"*The Sum of 4* is a *must* read if you want to find a new outlook on life and challenge yourself! I've been lucky enough to know Blue for most of my life, and this book truly captivates the reader, almost as much as his voice does!"

— Jean Luc Baker
Team USA Figure Skater

"Blue Stiley tells a compelling story that teaches, inspires, and gives the reader both insights into self-discovery and encouragement for finding a happier and more productive path forward. In a crowded field of self-improvement books, Stiley sets himself apart with his honest analysis, original thinking, and positive approach. He is humble, down to earth, trustworthy, and gives hope and conveys energy. A very fine work that will be valued by the reader and reread many times."

— Will F. Abrams
Consulting Professor, Stanford University
Attorney at Law, Schwabe Williamson & Wyatt

"In *The Sum of 4*, Blue Stiley uses his personal life experiences by providing useful action steps—*think* and *do*—that will challenge you in your efforts to be more successful. He provides clear recommendations on how to improve your daily life to enhance your performance and attitude, as well as others around you."

— Dr. Ernesto Ricardo S. ERSB, DDS
Clinical Professor Associate Dean, University of Washington

"Touching lives is the greatest gift. Blue Stiley shows us real-life experiences to help us open that gift."

— Cliff Hersman
CPA, JD Partner Hersman Serles Almond, PLLC

"Blue Stiley has inspired, trained, and motivated me for eighteen years. I met him training a client, and the energy between them was thunderous. It wasn't expectations of 'Do this,' but rather '*Do this*!' His banter wasn't just training, but absolutely motivational and inspirational. He has channeled that gift from the gym to the stage. He is a speaker you should hear and not miss! His life story and unique formula for reaching a desired result are life-changing messages."

— Dr. Ernie Barrett, DDS
Owner and Founder, 32 Good Reasons

"From the moment I met Blue Stiley, he impressed me. I knew I was meeting a force of nature. He had high energy, confidence, and immediately remembered everyone's name in the room. I have represented Blue as a fashion model for many years, and he is one of my favorites. Blue has a way of relating to others and has always been a positive and professional ambassador of our company, SMG. He overcomes all obstacles placed before him, and I can think of no one better to share lessons about leadership, mentoring, growth, and maximizing potential."

— Kristy Petersen
Co-Owner & Founder, Seattle Models Guild

"I have been a conditioning client of Blue's for sixteen years, and each time I work out with him, I'm impressed by his boundless energy and enthusiasm. In the process of building my strength, he inspires me to be a better person by sharing his wisdom, commitment to healthy living, and positive worldview. Our training sessions are the highlight of my week."

— Boyd Morrison
#1 *NY Times* bestselling author of *The ARK*

"For more than twenty years, Blue has grown from being my classmate, to my friend, my senpai, and my mentor. He has inspired me to take many chances that have truly catapulted my successes and my becoming the person I am today. This book and his proven strategies to finding the path that is best for you truly provide amazing insights into becoming the best you can be and how he has become a driving force in the lives of so many."

— Rufus McLain
Senior Director of Operations, Stitch Fix

"Blue has worked with me as a mentor, guide, coach, and friend for six years. He consistently challenges and inspires me to be my best and to face the challenges of life head-on. With humor and charm, but without ever being preachy or sappy, Blue helps me appreciate and tap into my own potential for greatness. I have witnessed him working with dozens of other people, and I believe his compassionate but firm guidance will benefit anyone. The experiences and insights he shares in this book are simply a reflection of who he is as a person: someone who genuinely loves and cares about people and instinctively makes everyone around him better."

— Matt Dubin
Founding Attorney of Dubin Law Group
Best-Selling Author of *Maximizing Your Injury Claim*

"Growing up with Blue as my athletic trainer, I understood and knew that in his classroom, the words 'I can't' meant and equated to doing many push-ups. Although this was a silly thing we would laugh about back then, it is just one of the many life habits Blue taught me as a mentor and trainer early in my life, which has stuck with me to this day. In *The Sum of 4*, Blue has done an amazing job of understanding the challenges we face as individuals in our day-to-day lives and has successfully articulated ways to think critically and how to take action. His book has reminded me to keep pushing forward and to always continue to grow!"

— Amanda Hofmann
US Figure Skating National Medalist
Risk and Fixed Income Derivative Specialist, Bloomberg LP

"Actions, not just the words, have made me look up to Blue Stiley. From our first hello, to where we are today, I've known that Blue's a man who walks the walk and talks the talk through passion, humility, kindness, and love. He's a true gentleman who changes the game in today's society. He leads by example. He's not afraid to make mistakes! He owns them and learns through them. He mentors through transparency. He's a god shot, and he is willing to take the ride."

— Gregory Zarian
Actor & Lifestyle Expert

"I first got to know Blue Stiley as a personal trainer. He has helped me achieve physical results I once only dreamed about. But more importantly, over the years, his mentoring, coaching, advice, and friendship have been an integral part of my development, both personally and professionally. Where I am today would not have been possible without Blue being a part of my life."

— Erik Schwedhelm
Boeing Marketing Director

"Blue Stiley's book, *The Sum of 4*, is a rare combination of practical, impactful, and insightful prose. His willingness to candidly and emotionally expose himself to the reader gains him instant credibility. Combine all these elements and add in the objective results, and you have a perfect recipe for success. A must read for anyone interested in pursuing greatness who understands the journey will be complicated, but worth all of the effort."

— Paul Richard Brown
Attorney at Law, Partner Karr Tuttle Campbell

"Blue is a connoisseur of learning and helping. After fifteen years, I have always remarked at his level of sincerity when he listens and acts. I have watched him develop his brand, which has not always been easy. As a friend, he has always been a positive inspiration. He shares his thoughts here, in this book, because he truly wants to see others succeed."

— Martin Williams
Federal Law Enforcement Officer

"If you want to be inspired, *The Sum of 4* does the job. Blue Stiley will share with you his remarkable story from being bullied as a child to becoming a fitness model, black belt, actor, and entrepreneur. Best of all, he'll provide you with a roadmap so you can equally achieve your own goals, whatever they may be. Don't miss this opportunity to learn from a master."

— Patrick Snow, Publishing Coach and
International Best-Selling Author of
Creating Your Own Destiny and *Boy Entrepreneur*

"Blue Stiley takes readers on a rollercoaster ride full of '80s nostalgia as well as hard-hitting truths and inspiration about what it takes to succeed in life. You will laugh. You will cheer. But best of all, you will come away changed and knowing how to continue to change for the better so you can achieve the things you most want in life."

— Tyler Tichelaar, PhD
Award-Winning Author of *The Best Place* and *Narrow Lives*

"Whether you are young or old, rich or poor, Blue will touch your life with his insights, wisdom, clarity, and depth of reasoning. His influence in my life has helped me define boundaries, live in the present moment, and realize my greatest power is the power of intention. Blue understands the power of intention, and he understands the power of living in the now. *The Sum of 4* teaches us the importance of surrounding ourselves with those who are conducive to our personal growth and momentum and then how to make that happen. Blue's awareness and concept of living abundantly, powerfully, and gracefully in the world is reflected in this book."

— Sandy Anderson
Real Estate Developer

"Blue Stiley's *The Sum of 4* tells the truth about what it takes to implement lasting change in your life. Through personal stories of how he overcame fear and achieved his own success, he creates a roadmap for the reader that will leave you inspired to conquer your obstacles and follow your dreams without looking back."

— Nicole Gabriel, Author of
Finding Your Inner Truth and *Stepping Into Your Becoming*

MENTOR · DEVELOP · EXECUTE · SUCCEED

THE SUM OF 4

THE SECRET EQUATION TO ACCELERATING ACHIEVEMENT

BLUE STILEY

Make today + everyday legendary!

The Sum of 4: The Secret Equation to Accelerating Achievement
Copyright © 2020 by Blue Stiley. All rights reserved.

Published by:
Aviva Publishing
Lake Placid, NY
(518) 523-1320
www.AvivaPubs.com

All Rights Reserved. No part of this book may be used or reproduced in any manner whatsoever without the expressed written permission of the author. Address all inquiries to:

Blue Stiley
blue@bluestiley.com
BlueStiley.com

ISBN: 978-1-950241-99-6
Library of Congress Control Number: 2020911557

Editors: Larry Alexander and Tyler Tichelaar, Superior Book Productions
Cover Design and Interior Book Layout: Nicole Gabriel
Author Photo: Mcklyn Cole Valenciano

Every attempt has been made to properly source all quotes.

Printed in the United States of America

To my wife, Heidi
My daughter, Haiden
The late Robey R. Reed, my karate and judo instructor
And my hippie parents, Patrick and Maureen Stiley
Thank you!

ACKNOWLEDGMENTS

Writing this book was harder than I thought, but more rewarding and enjoyable than I could have ever imagined. None of it would have been possible without the help and support of my wife, Heidi. I am especially grateful for her believing in me and encouraging me to literally write the next chapter in my life. From watching her laugh out loud and smile while reading my early drafts and outlines to pushing me to become a better man, father to our beautiful daughter, and husband, I have come to realize how written words cannot express how much you mean to me! "Only once." HNS.

To my daughter Haiden, who always seems to keep me and her mom on our toes. Your ability to make me smile from ear to ear is priceless, and I cherish that you enjoy *Star Wars,* possibly more than I do. "I love you a million plus one."

I'm eternally grateful to the late Robey R. Reed, my karate and judo instructor, who became the father figure I so desperately needed as a young boy. He is someone I would do 10,000 push-ups for if he ever asked. He taught me discipline, respect, patience, humility, confidence, and fearlessness. He helped me become more than I ever knew I could be. He taught me how to execute a lethal reverse punch and round-kick, and so much more that has helped me succeed in life. You are forever in my thoughts, Sensei.

To my hippie parents, Patrick and Maureen Stiley, who brought me into this world and gave me every opportunity to follow my passions. To my late dad, who introduced me to his own martial arts instructor, who then became my greatest mentor. To my mom, for always being the person I could turn to. Thank you, Mom, for never stopping me from doing what I loved, always challenging me to better myself, listening when I needed an ear, and offering to switch places anytime I was ever physically hurt. I am so thankful for you both.

To my childhood best friends, Adam and Moses, who have been copilots through most of my life. They stood by me during every struggle and were always there when I needed them. And a special thank you to Adam, who successfully challenged me to give up fast food, cold turkey, in high school. That is true friendship.

I'm indebted to my Japanese host sister, Risa Iwakura, for always being patient with my passion to learn Japanese and for helping me with my homework on the subway ride to school. You are truly a sister to me and part of my family.

A very special thanks to Kristy Peterson, who brought me on as an inexperienced model and actor at SMG Models. My time, longevity, and success in the industry wouldn't have been possible without you and your entire team's help and support, especially Mr. Camouflage himself, Andrew. Thank you!

Writing a book about the lessons I learned throughout my life is a surreal process. I'm forever indebted to Boyd and Randi Morrison for their editorial help, keen insight, guidance, friendship, and ongoing support in bringing my stories to life. Because of their efforts and encouragement, I have a written legacy to pass on to my family.

A big thanks to my speaking and book writing coach, Patrick Snow. Thank you for educating me on the dos and don'ts of becoming an author and keynote speaker.

Special thanks to my editing team at Superior Book Productions, Larry

Alexander and Tyler Tichelaar, for the excellent back and forth advice and feedback. Also, to my ever-patient cover designer Nicole Gabriel, for the hours of brainstorming and the amazing cover!

A very special thanks to my financial mentors, Cliff and Vicki. I'm honored to be treated like one of the family. Thank you for educating, supporting, and leading me toward a successful and financially intelligent future. Your faith in me and your support mean the world to me and my family.

To Ray Park, for all the inspiration and motivation to "keep kicking," eat my Weetabix, and follow the path to the Darkside. Thank you, brother.

Finally, this book has been shaped, guided, and supported by so many influential friends, teachers, coaches, and mentors. I am so thankful for the work and contributions of so many people who have served as mentors to me in some way. I'm honored and thankful to all those who have been a part of accomplishing my dreams and goals to live an enjoyable life and my getting there. Thanks to: my *Amazing Race* cousin in crime, Nick Stiley. Thanks also to Derek Madel, Ernest Barrett, Robert and Janine Dodson, Matt Dubin, Lawrence and Gregory Zarian, Darren Schell, Christophe Servieres "Big Jim," Rick Montgomery, Hope Misterek, Yvonne Castaneda, Tonya Sherman, Kevin Capuzzi, Rico, Rufus, Masayuki Tsunemine, "Mushi," Mike L., Martin Williams, Mandara, Dan Cooper, Lazarus Kawinga, Keri Armbruster, and to all my talent and modeling agencies.

CONTENTS

Introduction	23
PART I MENTOR	**31**
Chapter 1 The Power of Mentoring	33
Chapter 2 Introducing My Mentor	43
Chapter 3 Learning to Fall	55
Chapter 4 Building a Strong Foundation	67
PART II DEVELOP	**81**
Chapter 5 Encouraging Respect	83
Chapter 6 Creating an Emotional Connection	95
Chapter 7 Learning from Bad Examples	111
Chapter 8 Maintaining Focus	123
Chapter 9 Being Prepared	137
Chapter 10 Being Afraid	151
PART III EXECUTE	**165**
Chapter 11 Failing 101	167
Chapter 12 Embracing Criticism	179
Chapter 13 Leveraging Influence	191
Chapter 14 Adopting a Growth Mindset	203
Chapter 15 Never Quitting	217

PART IV SUCCEED	**231**
Chapter 16 Standing Your Ground	233
Chapter 17 Embracing Change and Setting Goals	249
Chapter 18 Turning Your Passion into Success	265
Chapter 19 Balancing Life	281
Chapter 20 Believing in Yourself	291
A Final Note	305
About the Author	311
About Blue Stiley's Leadership & Mentoring Coaching	313
Book Blue Stiley to Speak at Your Next Event	315

4

MENTOR • DEVELOP • EXECUTE • SUCCEED

INTRODUCTION

The result of adding two or more numbers is the definition of a sum. *The Sum of 4* is a concept that emphasizes the fact that there are multiple, if not infinite, ways to reach certain results, goals, dreams, or destinations. It's like the classic idiom: There is more than one way to cook an egg. Life is not a perfect template. We all learn and do things differently because no one is exactly the same. What works or resonates for me might not work or resonate for you. There is no single way of doing something, dealing with an obstacle, or overcoming a challenge. Accepting this theory and learning to effectively think outside the box, and in more than one way, is the strategy and methodology behind *The Sum of 4*. It is an easy four-step system, MENTOR, DEVELOP, EXECUTE, and SUCCEED, that if implemented correctly, will find your most efficient path to accelerating achievement.

Which one of these best describes your current personal and professional mood?

Life is flying by at "ludicrous speed." You hate not being able to successfully break away from the rest of the crowd; you feel stuck, unlucky, and like you're being left behind. This is not where you saw yourself at this point in your life. You want more in life; you are full of aspirations and dreams, but something is holding you back. You're at a crossroads and need a push in the right direction!

Or...

You regret choices in your past and feel like you've settled in multiple areas of your life. You no longer learn anything of value at work and you don't find it challenging. You want to improve your income level, move up the corporate ladder, or be more successful in your life. You want this, but you don't know what you're doing wrong or why you haven't been able to achieve these goals yet! You're looking for quick and real results, but the learning curve seems endless. You are looking for a competitive edge or that magic pill!

If you can relate to or identify with any of the above, you are not alone. I understand first-hand the pressures you feel as a parent, student, recent graduate, employee, employer, business owner, entrepreneur, salesman, or instructor. I know what it is like to be afraid of the unknown or to take chances in life. I know how hard it is to be an outsider and ask for help, go back to school, learn or try new and difficult things, make lifestyle changes, and live in physical pain after multiple surgeries. I've made every excuse I can think of, felt every emotion possible, and kicked the responsibility can down the road for miles.

I know how you feel because I have been there and experienced the same challenges. However, the harsh reality that applies to everyone is: No one owes you anything in this world. No one is going to wave a magic wand to provide solutions and solve everything for you. It is up to you to find a way through life's challenges and obstacles in order to reach your goals and dreams. If you don't, you run the risk of being in the same place in the future that you are now. By the end of this book, you will know the secret equation and winning formula to accelerating your achievement, and we will do it together.

THERE IS A NEED

Life lessons and the practice of respecting and demanding more of ourselves and humanity, which used to be passed down generation to generation by our parents and their parents before them, seems to have skipped a few recent decades or generations. People are not learning these values from their jobs, schools, religions, or families. Something is missing!

Part of the problem is that we, as humans, are creatures of routine and habit. We fear change so we become comfortable, content, and lazy, and we begin to settle in all aspects of our daily lives. Somewhere along the way, we lose focus, give up on our dreams, become weighed down with responsibilities, make excuses, and procrastinate. Even though the world is changing, many of us cease to craft and master ourselves. Life is an uphill battle, where most of us have forgotten or never learned how to effectively improve ourselves to save time, money, and energy.

Granted, a small minority of us do not suffer from these frustrations and are naturals when dealing with personal or professional obstacles and roadblocks. Such people either figure out how to successfully navigate problems by themselves or they know how to reach out, hire, team up, or associate with others who know how. Unfortunately, most of us are not so lucky or intuitive when it comes to dealing with life's challenges. Therein lies the gap that needs fixing!

In my experience, those less fortunate either don't have a pool of talented people around them, or they are averse to seeking out and surrounding themselves with positive influencers who can raise them out of this rut. With the explosion of social media, certainly no shortage exists of inspirational self-help personalities, bloggers, or lifestyle enthusiasts with millions of followers, all preaching the same message about how to live a positive and confident life. Why these personalities or brands fall short of truly motivating and inspiring others, however, is they miss the ability to truly relate or connect with someone.

Following a personality online or merely meeting someone is one thing, but truly connecting with a person who significantly and positively propels and influences one's life or trajectory is another. Just being in the vicinity of talented and successful people doesn't necessarily translate or equate to you becoming more talented and successful yourself either. There needs to be a cause or catalyst to elevate and spark a change in your growth and momentum. What truly guides and reinforces our ability to develop and master the skills required to "get more and expect more" of ourselves, and our peers, communities, and society, is the connection.

In this book, I will introduce you to when I was bullied as a child and how a specific confrontation became a life-changing event for me. It served as a catalyst to meet a certain key figure who taught me the secret ingredient to overcoming the basic obstacles to achieving great success in my work and personal life. His life lessons, habits to live by, and mentorship taught me not only to deal with the bully, but how to apply the power of being effectively mentored to catapult and achieve my natural best. This process set into motion my designing and creating an easy and proven program for others to yield the same results and accelerate their learning!

This book is for anyone who wants more out of life. It's for those who want to turn their dreams and goals into reality and control their future. You don't have to enjoy, love, or even know anything about martial arts to learn from this book. You also don't have to be a child of the '70s or '80s to relate to it. It's for the underdog who has always had to hustle, work hard, and overcome self-doubt to get ahead. This book is for anyone who wants to upgrade themselves, boost their career, save time and money, and strengthen their mind. It's for those who don't want to miss the personal growth train about to depart the station.

My mission is to use a collection of inspirational and humorous real-life stories and proven strategies I was mentored in to create the personal equation and system for you to turn your dreams and goals into reality. Whether it is your work, business, health, finances, or relationships, this method will develop the guideposts to produce the winning formula required to achieve who you were meant to be in record time.

Discovering the formula to accelerate my success did not happen overnight. I have been refining and adapting it for more than thirty years. One lesson at a time, my journey has been a constant quest to learn and better understand more efficient ways to help students, audiences, clients, and executives gain the traction required to achieve greater success. From getting my first business license at the age of twelve and graduating with multiple degrees to learning to speak several languages, working abroad, maintaining a twenty-year international acting and modeling career, and coaching and mentoring thousands of clients and students worldwide as a professional mentor, personal trainer, professional keynote speaker, martial arts instructor, and now author, I have been blessed to learn from many great mentors. Thirty years of experiences, challenges, and lessons add up to tens of thousands of hours of hands-on planning, teaching, coaching, mentoring, facilitating, and solving real life problems. *The Sum of 4* is the culmination of all this hard work.

My typical coaching client is growth-oriented, wants to shorten their learning curve for reaching their goals and dreams, is hungry for change, wants more in life, and is willing to face some harsh realities to improve their lives. If this describes you, then you're reading the right book and have everything you need. You won't need to spend countless hours, months, or years mastering specific skills. Instead, you're going to learn to change your mindset or way of thinking. You're going to discover and develop a specific and personalized formula to getting what you most want in life.

Although this book contains lessons and strategies I learned throughout

28   THE SUM OF 4

my life, they are easy to implement and follow to transform you into the person you want to be. I will end each chapter with a "think" and "do" assignment to uncover the most effective method for you to control your own destiny. Each chapter will also end with an example of a successful famous mentor/mentee relationship to emphasize the value of modeling an expert with extensive knowledge who offers their help and is already getting the results you want.

I understand why you haven't yet reached the success and heights you have wished and dreamed of. I, too, am out there every day, working with my own mentors and clients, constantly applying, testing, and proving that these skills and tools work. This book is a roadmap, with a formula or "way of life" to getting you the results you want. Once applied, these practical and universal principles will fast-track you to reaching your goals. I have tremendous respect for you because I know you are someone who wants and expects more for yourself. You are not alone.

Are you ready to compress decades and years of knowledge and experience into months and days? Ready to bring out the best in yourself and others, navigate the challenges we all face, become more successful, and achieve your life goals and dreams? If the answer is yes, then please don't let this book collect dust. I encourage you to trust me, continue turning the pages, and let me motivate, inspire, and become your virtual mentor as you navigate through my shared lessons. In what is to follow, you might just find something that was missing, discover your hidden talents and abilities, and be slightly entertained. It's time to buckle your seatbelt and hit the success accelerator!

Best wishes for your successful journey.

Blue Stiley

PART I
MENTOR

THE SUM OF 4

MENTOR • DEVELOP • EXECUTE • SUCCEED

CHAPTER 1

THE POWER OF MENTORING

"My job is not to be easy on people. My job is to take these great people we have and to push them and make them even better."

— Steve Jobs

A DREAM

The windows were so steamed from the inside that any bystander passing by the old, red-brick building, which was once a giant used record store, wouldn't be able to see the focus and intensity of the thirty or so people inside. The room smelled of sweat, much like a high school locker room in the middle of summer. The dampness in the air could be felt from the sweat that poured from everyone's arms and legs as they performed defense drills time after time after time. "*Ichi, Ni, San*...!" the class would yell out in Japanese while executing specific techniques.

It must have been more than a hundred degrees inside the dojo. The bamboo *tatami* mats were slippery from the sweat dripping from the students' legs and forearms. The students' focus, including mine, was so intense you could hear a pin drop on the mat as we prepared to deliver our next round of front kicks, which, when they connected with the heavily worn, black punching pads, made the sound of a hundred whips snapping in midair simultaneously. One could easily write their name with their finger on the steam-covered mirrors running horizontally down the mat.

Our karate instructor paced back and forth like a shark in shallow water looking for prey, ready to lunge the moment a baby seal lost focus. With well over an hour left of class, we were already exhausted from the initial twenty-minute endurance warm-up we had just begun.

While we stood in line, you could see the anguish in our faces as the fatigue began to take its toll. It felt as if our nervous systems had nothing left to give. Our quadriceps shook and our heels uncontrollably tapped the mat in rhythmic motions like a jack hammer as we executed the kicks. If allowed, we would have jumped at the opportunity for a short water break, not only for our muscles to regain control, but to rehydrate our parched, dry mouths.

Despite the hot and humid weather outside, a slight breeze trickled in from a slightly cracked window in the back of the room. Unfortunately, this breeze did nothing to stop perspiration from accumulating on my forehead and dripping into my eyes, causing them to burn and forcing me to wipe them repeatedly with the canvas-style sleeve of my already sweat-stained and soaked white uniform.

With my eyes still painfully stinging, I tried to securely plant my feet, for traction, but my heels continued to slip. To say I was leaking like a sieve would be a major understatement. A giant puddle began to form directly beneath my stance. I needed to stop and/or slow the chronic "leak" from my body and somehow dry myself before I or someone else slipped in the small pond I was creating. Careful not to distract our instructor or the entire class, I quietly asked a classmate to use his sweat towel.

Understanding the situation's urgency, my classmate handed me the towel. Despite my good intentions and asking covertly, losing focus on the task at hand and distracting my classmate was the wrong choice, according to our instructor, whose disapproval was immediate.

With demon eyes, our instructor turned and screamed, "You two...10,000 knuckle push-ups!" Panic brought me an immediate rush of adrenaline, and with it, strength. Without missing a beat, we both dropped down and began whittling away at the 10,000 repetitions demanded.

And then, just like that, I awoke from the nightmare.

IF EVERYONE JUMPED OFF THE CLIFF...

Being told to do something only done in some sadistic Navy SEAL training course was only a dream. But was what happened in this dream really that horrible or far from how I would act in reality?

The truth is, if my karate instructor asked me to do 10,000 knuckle push-ups, I would have begun doing them without hesitation. I would not have complained, argued, or tried to negotiate, nor would I have quit or thrown a grown-up tantrum. It is human nature to question everything, but the reality is I would have just followed direction as I did in my nightmare. However, simple obedience, just to do what others are doing, like the popular myth that small lemming rodents unknowingly follow each other off cliffs to their sure death, is not why I would just follow his instructions either.

I ask myself, *Why would I just start doing 10,000 push-ups? How would he get me to do something that seemed so miserable and nearly impossible?* The answer is simple. I respected, trusted, and loved this man—not only as my instructor but as my mentor. He willingly encouraged and guided me—sharing his knowledge, skills, and experience—to advance not only my own martial arts skills, but my life and career. In my opinion, that is the core definition of mentoring, and exemplifies its overwhelming power to positively influence another.

Webster's Dictionary defines *mentor* as: a. A trusted counselor or guide, or b. Tutor or coach.

Bob Proctor, one of the world's most highly regarded speakers on prosperity, inspiration, and motivation, once defined a mentor as "someone who sees more talent and ability within you than you see in yourself and helps bring it out of you."

Proctor's definition of a mentor is precisely correct. A great mentor will point out what they think the mentee should and could do better, how the mentee can improve and polish their skills, and what action is required to solve their problem. They will know how to draw a mentee out of their comfort zone and push them toward setting up a specific plan to improve themselves—one they can easily understand and follow.

Imagine if you could go back in time to meet your old self for a heart-to-heart chat. What would you tell yourself? What advice, direction, or encouragement would you give? What pitfalls or mistakes would you warn yourself against? Besides which stocks to buy or bets to make, you'd have some incredibly valuable and wise bits of information and connections to share with your past self—all of which would really help you navigate your future for years to come.

You would believe and trust yourself. Not only would your future self have a vested interest in the results and your achievements, but your past self would vehemently trust and respect the source. You wouldn't think twice about following your own advice because your wiser self knows more and has your best interests in mind. How awesome would that be?

This is the definition and power of a key mentor: someone who has been there, can walk you through things, has already gotten the results you want, can compress decades and years of knowledge into days, is happy for you when you succeed, and brings out your natural best. They also believe in you and have a great relationship and connection with you.

Anyone can be a leader or influencer, but that does not mean they are effective, strong, and/or truly influential. A great mentor, on the other hand, is made or followed through by choice, love, trust, and admiration—a great mentor makes us want to mimic them. Not every leader is a mentor, but every mentor is a natural leader. The difference is in the relationship. With a mentor, there is an absolute relationship based on trust, empathy, and respect.

Mentors and leaders are similar because both can add value to your life and/or career, but for a leader to be a mentor, they must give of themselves. This takes true intent by the leader. Here is what global business guru and author Bob Goshen once said about what a great leader does: "Leaders should influence others in such a way that builds people up, encourages, and educates them so they can duplicate this attitude in others." This is the same meaning as that of a great mentor!

Mentoring focuses on developing the mentee's skills and confidence. It is more relationship- than performance- or numbers-based. The common thread in all successful mentoring relationships is a meaningful connection. Mentoring effectively takes leaders and adds a real connection and sense of value. This addition allows a leader to be more effective because the employee/mentee wants to follow them. Without a mentor or great leader's support, you might as well be standing still on a moving walkway. Eventually, you'll get from one point to the next. but with the support of a mentor, it's like you are walking or even sprinting. A mentor will accelerate your journey faster than you can ever do it alone.

Whether the missing ingredient to securing success is supplied by a parent, mentor, teacher, pastor, community leader, or, in my case, a martial arts instructor, it comes from someone who uses words like accountability, integrity, engagement, intention, commitment, vision, and excellence in defining action steps. The specifics don't matter. Nor does the age or experience of your mentor. Everyone has a story to tell, and anyone you can learn from through advice, insights, or experience can and should be your mentor.

I could not do what I am doing, have what I have, have been able to make the sacrifices I've made, or continue breaking through every goal I have set without the help of those around me who had more knowledge and experience or greater expertise. What matters most is what you do with that new learned knowledge, and that the connection is meaningful and provides the balance you need to become the best you can be!

MENTOR/MENTEE

Former Apple Inc.'s CEO, the late Steve Jobs, mentored Facebook's CEO, Mark Zuckerberg, for many years. They shared a similar background as young, driven entrepreneurs. When Jobs met

Zuckerberg, Jobs mentored, advised, and shared many insights and ideas about innovative technology with Zuckerberg, who knew having someone to turn to for advice and guidance was key to transforming his business, especially in Facebook's early stages. When Jobs passed away, Zuckerberg wrote, "Steve, thank you for being a mentor and a friend. Thanks for showing that what you build can change the world. I will miss you."

SUMMARY

By adopting the principles and lessons that follow in this book, as I once did, you will create the personal power to change all your old behaviors and control your own destiny. If you do not like the dream you are in, it is time to wake up and take back control and change! You need a strong will and desire to adopt these principles and strategies. But if you can apply them to your life, the transformation will be obvious. Instead of blindly "following the leader," you will create a new dream—one you are in control of and can change on your terms.

ACTION STEPS

THINK

Knowing what you know now, what would you do differently if you could live your life over?

_____

_____

_____

_____

List the five most influential, inspirational, and motivational people in your life.

_____

_____

_____

_____

_____

Name at least one thing you can positively attribute to something they did or said.

_____

_____

If you could meet any two successful or famous mentors, who would they be? Who do you know right now, within your circle, whom you can ask to be your mentor?

1. _____

2. _____

DO

Learn from others to drastically speed up the learning curve. You will save a lot of time, money, and energy if you learn from someone who has gotten and continues to get the results you want.

Make a habit of asking yourself, "Who would know or have expertise about this?" "Who could guide or teach me how to master this?"

Make an effort to reach one or both of the famous or most successful mentors you'd like to meet!

Align yourself with the two people you envision could be great mentors in your inner circle, and ask them if they are willing to offer any guidance, advice, or knowledge to propel your life forward.

Immediately contact your mentor or an influential person in your life to check in with them and give them an update. Let them know they have positively changed and impacted you. Ask if there is something you can do for them.

THE SUM OF 4

MENTOR · DEVELOP · EXECUTE · SUCCEED

CHAPTER 2
INTRODUCING MY MENTOR

"Each of us must confront our own fears, must come face to face with them. How we handle our fears will determine where we go with the rest of our lives. To experience adventure or to be limited by the fear of it."

— Judy Blume

As I mentioned in the last chapter, as humans, we face all kinds of challenges, fears, and uncertainties throughout our lives. While we go through these phases, we should seek advice and be open to support from those who reach out. This support helps us navigate and manage obstacles naturally. One must willingly ask for support and guidance or be ready to accept it when someone willingly offers it. A great mentorship should be natural and organic.

This chapter will introduce you to my childhood and the story of how, as a result of being bullied, I came to meet my greatest mentor. Looking back, are there certain situations or impactful moments you can credit with forming who you are, what you believe, or why you act a certain way? Can you vividly recall that moment or how you felt? Our senses are so powerful, connecting us to this world and helping shape our memories. Simply remembering a person, event, smell, or situation can trigger happiness, frustration, anger, jealousy, pain, grief, uncertainty, or even a sudden rush of fear.

I GREW UP IN A HAUNTED MANSION

I was born in Spokane, Washington, in the late 1970s. My parents, Maureen and Patrick Stiley, were both "hippies to the bone." This was a factor to the choice of my name. Blue is my given name—no awards for thinking I have a dog name or quoting the movie *Old School*, "You're my boy, Blue!"

My mom was a stay-at-home mom, while my dad worked as a defense attorney, specializing in drug, and labor and industry cases. As an only child, I lived on the South Hill in Spokane, two blocks from my elementary school, in an old and poorly maintained house many people said was and still is haunted. Boo! I was raised in what is known as "The Hahn Mansion," a twenty-six-plus room (give or take the hidden rooms) "haunted" mansion. It has been the inspiration for multiple news articles about mysterious deaths, creepy sounds, and even possible buried treasure somewhere in or around the home. Whether the ghost stories and hidden treasure are fact or fiction, I feel very lucky to have called The Hahn Mansion home.

Don't be fooled; just because we lived in a "mansion," doesn't mean we had money. We had a lot of space for the three of us, but the house was poorly maintained, most rooms were eerily empty, and the fancy decor was definitely missing. It certainly wasn't Pinterest worthy, with or without ghosts.

Living an opulent life, acquiring wealth, and working in personal finance were beyond my parents' understanding. Wealth and money were never important to either of them. All of life's necessities were taken care of, but they believed in generosity and sharing. And my parents certainly knew how to find bargains. Not to knock

Kmart, but as a kid, I could recite any blue light special.

The family manor, nor my unique first name, did not exactly win me any cool kid awards. The combination made me an easy target for bullies, much like Johnny Cash's song, "A Boy Named Sue."

BEING BULLIED

I was especially targeted by one specific kid who disliked me and lived between my house and my elementary school. On the way to and from school, up-hill both ways, of course, I usually crossed this unsavory character's path. He was known for picking on younger and smaller kids in the neighborhood, and I was one of his favorite targets. So much so that I intentionally took the long way home most days.

This happened more than thirty years ago, but I still vividly remember my fear. Each encounter I believed would be the one in which I was beaten senseless. He would corner and threaten me; I would nearly wet myself—which, in hindsight, could have been "the perfect self-defense." Who wants to fight a kid with wet pants, right?

Basically, it felt like a scene from the movie *A Christmas Story*, when Ralphie Parker and his brother Randy pass by the bully Scut Farkus on the way to and from school. If you are not familiar with this film, wow—making it through every Christmas since its release in 1983 without seeing it is an amazing feat. Anyway, Ralphie is the main character who, along with his brother and friends, occasionally encounters two neighborhood bullies. Ralphie eventually stands up to them. During one of Ralphie's first encounters, the film's narrator informs the viewer that the bully is not only very scary and intimidating but that, "He had yellow eyes...so help me, God, yellow eyes."

Well, my neighborhood bully didn't have yellow eyes, but at the age of eight, he scared me to death the day he told me he'd kill me.

That evening over dinner, I talked to my parents about how the confrontations had become increasingly more intense. I stressed that I believed in my heart that in the next encounter, I would truly be hurt physically. I described unsuccessful and pitiful attempts to de-escalate the situation by pleading, begging, and even bribing him, which only seemed to make it worse. I was at a loss how to escape the torment and overcome my painful fear. My mom said I should walk away even after I explained I had not only walked away but run away many times. My dad calmly interjected, "I have the solution."

Surely, as a professional litigator, my dad's solution would be a superb and foolproof way to negotiate with the bully. However, I had to wait a week to realize my father's solution, while using alternate and less convenient routes to school to avoid any confrontations. In the end, it wasn't so much a solution, as an introduction. My father introduced me to the man who would eventually teach me the lasting lessons and habits I needed to gain a competitive edge, develop confidence and self-leadership skills, and face any fear, including my childhood bully.

NINJA WANNABE

The following Saturday morning, with one stale glazed doughnut in my stomach, I jumped into our old van (without seatbelts) and my dad and I set off for a secret destination. Once on the road, he told me we were headed to a judo tournament at a local college.

Now, let me remind everyone that in the early '80s, an expedition

INTRODUCING MY MENTOR   47

to a judo tournament was like a dream come true for a boy. Ninjas, karate, judo, and Japan were the absolute rage back then. Everything—movies, cartoons, books, magazines, music, fashion, and video games—helped popularize Japan. Go team Atari and ColecoVision!

My adrenaline level was off the charts. To say I was giddy would be an understatement. I was so excited to be introduced to anything Japanese that I forgot all about my normal Saturday morning cartoon routine and the reason for our trip.

Once parked, I did everything not to bust open the car door and run through the parking lot like a wildebeest toward the last watering hole in the Serengeti. People inside the main entrance were busier than happy ants climbing over an unfortunate kid's dropped ice cream sandwich. The linoleum hallway was lined with vendor tables filled with cheap imitation weapons. It was what every American eight-year-old boy dreamed of.

I was in heaven! These were the things you saw in Chuck Norris, Bruce Lee, and Sho Kosugi movies. I began envisioning myself scaling steep walls dressed in a black ninja outfit. I even pictured wearing the strange, two-toed (*tabi*) boots the ninjas wore. Grappling hooks, knifes, swords, uniforms, throwing stars, belts, books, even blow guns with darts. Are you kidding me? Real blow guns! I can't begin to imagine how many house pets endured mysterious needle pricks from imaginative kids with blow guns. You name it, this place was selling it. Oh, how I miss the good old '80s. I also yearned for my piggy bank because, with the purchase of these weapons, I could devise my own plan for confronting my bully.

Volunteers were busy registering and signing in contestants for the tournament. Many of the contestants wore thick white pajama-style uniforms, each with different color belts wrapped around their waists. Some even had on blue uniforms. At that point, I had no idea of the colored belts and uniforms' significance. All I knew from the movies was not to mess with anyone wearing a black belt.

We bought two tickets and entered a gym that smelled like a combination of athletic tape, menthol, and an old medicine cabinet. Even though hundreds of people were jammed onto the fifteen-foot-high wooden bleachers surrounding the gym, it didn't seem disorganized. The floor was divided into four different sections, each with its own tricolored mat.

Each mat had a set of judges, tables with time clocks, rolodex scoring cards, red sashes like those used for flag football, and spectators completely surrounding it. Each section had two competitors who stood, bowed, and then started throwing each other down like ragdolls. They rolled around on the mat like a giant cobra grappling with a lightning-fast mongoose. It was very similar to a high school wrestling match, minus the nylon singlet and head gear.

MEETING MY MENTOR

My dad and I sat in the bleachers watching match after match for over an hour. Then, during a brief intermission, my father led me to the locker rooms. He directed me to a man at the end of the hall, standing in front of a collegiate trophy case filled with memorabilia from decades earlier. The stranger and my dad said hello, and then my dad formally introduced us.

The man was a foot shorter than my dad and just about a foot taller than me. What he lacked in height, he made up for in girth—he

INTRODUCING MY MENTOR 49

looked like the trunk of a redwood tree—thick, not an ounce of fat. His heather-gray slacks, shoeless feet with black socks, and navy-blue blazer with a crest sewn on his breast pocket seemed to form perfectly to his muscular physique.

And this man's hands—they were like a large bunch of hard bananas that, if curled into a fist, turned into a giant's club straight out of the classic fantasy roleplaying game *Dungeons and Dragons*.

"Blue," my father said, "this was my judo instructor in college, Technical Sergeant Robey R. Reed, but you can address him as Reed Sensei." This "Mr. Solid-as-a-Brick, Sensei Guy" introduced himself and said, "Pleasure to meet you, Blue. I hear you're being bullied."

First off, I thought, *What the heck is a sensei?* And second, *How did this guy know I was being bullied?* Obviously, my dad had called him. But I had never even heard of him.

In case you don't know, a *sensei* is a martial arts teacher or instructor.

In *Star Wars* terms, the Sith and Jedi had senseis and students. For example, Emperor Palpatine (sensei) had his apprentices (students) Darth Maul and Darth Vader. Master Yoda (sensei) had his young padawan (student) Obi Wan Kenobi. Yes, I'm an uber *Star Wars* fan, but I hope this analogy has helped.

Although I was eight at the time, my first meeting with Reed Sensei still feels like yesterday. Everything about this memory stands out vividly in my mind, including his black socks staring at me. I'm not sure if his socks stood out because my head was drooped down out of shame of being bullied or because I couldn't comprehend why a man would be dressed to a tee, yet be missing dress shoes. Turns out that judo judges, like the Japanese who remove their shoes when entering a home, remove them before getting on a mat.

Reed Sensei, in his captivating black socks and arms directly to his sides, kept constant eye contact while he listened intently to my fear of being humiliated and annihilated by the bully. When I was finished, he ever so warmly and slowly, and I mean sloth slow, leaned in toward me and softly said, "I believe you are too young to understand this, but running from your fears will never ever solve them; only by facing them head on with your head will a fear be resolved. It would be my honor to show you how to stand up against any fear, and teach you to punch and kick, but you must first learn how to fall and get back up."

And "learn to fall," I did....

MENTOR/MENTEE

Well known as "The Coach," both on and off the college football field, Bill Campbell played a big role in advising Apple's Steve Jobs and Google's co-founder Larry Page. He emphasized investing and empowering people to be creative. He believed CEOs should be closely involved in managing their companies. Even though Jobs and Page are the most successful in their specific fields, they attribute their successes to surrounding themselves with people who can push them and make them better, especially Bill Campbell.

SUMMARY

I was completely unaware that the man I had just met would change my life forever. He wasn't wearing a name tag to identify himself or his expertise in mentorship. Only in retrospect did I come to recognize the role he would play in my journey. There was no obvious flashing billboard stating the importance of this relationship or how he would help shape my life regarding my career and personal path to success. Because of my circumstances, I just happened to meet the right person at the right time.

At any moment, anyone you encounter could become your most influential mentor or you could possibly become theirs. Similarly, at no specific time, someone you already know or haven't met yet will play a significant role in your life. Some will be simple supporting roles; others might just be quick encounters. All are important events because you never know whom you will meet, what hidden talent they may unearth in you, or what you may be able to advise or inspire within them.

ACTION STEPS

THINK

How did you deal with a time you felt bullied or cornered as a kid? As an adult?

_____

_____

Can you name something important or difficult that happened to you that you didn't know how to overcome or manage by yourself? Something you needed outside advice or guidance about?

_____

_____

Whom have you met randomly who made a lasting difference or turned out to be a key influence in your life?

_____

_____

Whom have you've influenced as a positive role model? If so, did they tell you that you had?

_____

DO

Every time you meet someone, they have the potential to become your mentor or make a significant difference in your life. Imagine how or what you can learn from them. Embrace every friendship, relationship, and encounter as if they are a potential mentor. Even if it's only for a few minutes, be open to learning or sharing something with them.

Always ask yourself what you can learn from each person you meet.

THE SUM OF 4

MENTOR • DEVELOP • EXECUTE • SUCCEED

CHAPTER 3
LEARNING TO FALL

"He who would learn to fly one day must first learn to stand and walk and run and climb and dance; one cannot fly into flying."

— Friedrich Nietzsche

The last chapter reminded us to align ourselves with a mentor and always be open to meeting new people and building relationships. Any person you meet could turn out to be an amazing mentor, but you would never know it if you were not open to the experience. They may facilitate and propel your personal growth by providing the key to unlocking hidden talents and/or offering invaluable advice or connections to reach heights you think are impossible.

This chapter focuses on the importance of patience and how it is not only about waiting, but also about keeping a positive attitude while doing so. Learning from others can speed up your progress in gaining experience and new skills, but the results are not always immediate. A normal learning curve takes time—a whole lot of time. Normal or accelerated, you still have to ask yourself what your patience level is. Do you get bored easily, need instant gratification, become easily frustrated, give up on projects, or quit something because it took more time and effort than you initially thought?

PATIENCE

For all you "Hair Nation" fans, I apologize in advance that this section isn't about one of Guns N' Roses most popular songs. True fans, please whistle and hum away as you continue reading.

Patience is the ability to remain untroubled by life's changes, delays, or other undesirables. It's the ability to maintain stillness amid disappointment. Bill Gates, Microsoft's co-founder and one of the richest men in world, once said of patience, "Patience is a key element to success."

When you look at what it means to have patience, you are ultimately talking about dealing with your own thoughts and emotions. By cultivating a practice of patience, you can live with less stress, anxiety, and frustration. You're able to accept the things outside of your control or accommodate a new timeline. With patience, you are in the driver's seat and can dictate the speed of your life.

However, the ability to postpone or wait for all your wants, needs, and desires is not easy to develop. Our society's high-speed pace comes with a hectic and rushed focus on our careers, families, schooling, sports, and even health and wellness. We want it all, and we want it now. It's human nature to want more family time, be in better shape, have a better-paying job, get rapid promotions and raises, or want to make a difference in the world.

Putting in enough time and work to gain the necessary credentials and skills is what the learning process is all about. It can reap the greatest benefits and most rewarding experiences for the student. When we are in a rush to do and have everything now, we set ourselves up for failure, mentally and physically. We begin to forget what's most important to us and why we started on this journey.

Whether the cause is a short attention span, commitment issues, or a fear of missing out, you can avoid costly mistakes by simply practicing patience.

Oprah Winfrey didn't become one of the richest and most successful women in the United States overnight. She patiently and painstakingly mastered her skills by putting in the hard work, hustle, and determination required to climb the ladder. She highlighted the importance of patience when she said, "You can have it all. Just not all at once."

What Oprah so perfectly brings to light is that patience is required to become truly successful and proficient at anything. Success first takes a willingness to go slowly, literally and figuratively. Any professional athlete or subject matter expert will tell you that slowing down is the key to success. Whether it is parenting, athletics, coaching, or business, we all must learn to crawl before we walk.

Slowing down the movement and pace helps the mind and body get in tune with how it's supposed to feel and work. Going slow and spreading things out allows your mind to process them successfully while in a safe, controlled, and less chaotic environment. Having the patience to practice and put the time in to learn the basics allows everything to become second nature. Remember the process of learning to drive? I bet driving at high speeds, while merging on the freeway, now feels natural.

LEARNING TO FALL

Following my brief introduction to judo at the tournament, my parents decided to enroll me in a judo class. Classes were two nights a week, fifteen-minutes from home. My first session couldn't come fast enough—I felt like a kid waiting to open presents on Christmas morning. I rushed home after school, not even worrying about running into my neighborhood nemesis, to make sure I wasn't late to my first class. I was pumped and ready to walk through the doors of this mysterious place called a dojo and instantly become a ninja master.

But first, let's look at what exactly a dojo is. Yes, it's a school where martial arts are taught, but after thirty years of training in mostly Japanese martial arts, I define a dojo as a place where we begin to understand ourselves more fully, including who we are, how we react, what we fear, and how we handle conflict. It's a place to attempt new and difficult things while training the spirit, mind, and body—a place where patience, dedication, and discipline can break down the real world into manageable, bite-sized pieces by instilling true patience and discipline.

Not knowing what I would learn my first day, my imagination went wild. Would I master gymnastic flips like an Olympic gold medalist? Perform spin kicks like Chuck Norris did in his movies? Or maybe how to move my hands and feet with the glow and quickness of Bruce Lee? And lastly, would wearing a new judo uniform and belt automatically make me invincible?

Nope, none of that was right—zero, zilch, nada!

Instead, just as Reed Sensei had mentioned, I learned to fall. Literally!

There were no acrobatic cartwheels, no spinning jump kicks, and certainly no egg-beater style arm or leg movements. And unless you call the well-worn Optimus Prime T-shirt and tan Cub Scout shorts I was wearing a uniform, the cool uniform with a black belt was a big fat "No" as well! I seemed to have forgotten what Reed Sensei initially said about learning "to fall first" before learning the "cool" stuff. Oops.

First, I didn't know that one doesn't start out kicking or striking in judo until one is well advanced. Second, most kids quit martial arts soon after their initial class. Therefore, many instructors suggest waiting to buy a uniform for a month or so to make sure it is a good fit (pun intended).

Just like wearing a pair of Air Jordans wouldn't make me jump higher, wearing a uniform didn't make me a master martial artist. Reality began to sink in, and for me, it was like Bill (Keanu Reeves) often said during his and Ted's excellent adventure, "Bogus."

When my dad and I entered the dojo, we were immediately hit by frigidly cold air in what smelled like a clean and sterile operating room. I was already nervous, and the cold room added to the goose bumps already covering my body. The temperature made me wish I had worn my matching Transformers sweatpants instead of those shorts. Once my dad and I filled out the paperwork, I was assigned an older student who would serve as my upperclassman or what is known as a senpai. He would be responsible for teaching me the basic dos and don'ts of judo and dojo etiquette.

With my shoes and socks off, I followed my senpai's lead by bowing at the edge of the mat before stepping on it. We joined a dozen or so others already stretching and practicing various techniques on the mat. We began to warm up, and my senpai explained we would soon line up by rank, as indicated by the color of the belts, in descending order behind the black belts.

As class began, everyone hustled to line up with complete fluidity and efficiency—no wasted motion. Everyone knew their place and lined up! That is, of course, everyone except the skinny fifty-five-pound, eight-year-old "sticks with lips" me in my vintage pajama wear.

I seriously looked like a young fawn caught in a semi truck's headlights, watching helplessly as everyone systematically formed a straight line near the edge of the mat. A moment later, my senpai ushered me to the end of the line, with all the white belts.

Our instructor and the highest ranked black belts lined up in front of us, while the "new kid on the mat" sat at the end of the line wearing extremely short shorts. Having no idea what to do, I played "monkey see, monkey do." This served me very well, especially since the beginning of class and most of the instructions were in Japanese.

My lack of coordination was instantly apparent. Watching my inability to use different parts of my body together smoothly and efficiently was like watching a cat with Popsicle sticks taped to its legs! I felt like the kid who grew twelve inches in a single summer and was having trouble with simple tasks like putting one foot in front of the other (aka walking). Attempting to follow the instructions in Japanese made me feel like I'd just been thrown into a salad mix. But I figured since I didn't learn to ride my bike in one day, my coordination and language skills had some time to catch up as well.

After completing several fast-paced stretches and joint rotations in directions only contortionists should bend, I joined my senpai in one of the corners of the mat. He said it was time to learn and practice the "break-fall." I wondered if we were about to learn a new break dance move. Remember, it was the early '80s, so in my mind, it was quite possible I would be learning to successfully defeat Michael Jackson's moonwalk in a dance off.

What followed certainly wasn't The Centipede dance. Instead, I began to "learn to fall." Reed Sensei wasn't kidding when he said I needed to "learn to fall before learning to kick." First off, I had no idea I didn't know how to fall already. I mean, I was a pretty clumsy kid, so the act of falling seemed exceptionally self-explanatory to me. One minute you're up, and the next, you find yourself on the floor, usually with a terror-filled screech thrown in somewhere. And second, I didn't know there was more than one way to fall. That evening, I was introduced to falls forward, backward, sideways, while upside down, with great speed, rolling in any direction, by surprise, from heights, or while being thrown like a rag doll by a well-trained judo practitioner.

In judo, among other martial arts, all beginners learn how to fall properly before they do any kind of throwing. Through these falling drills, known as *ukemi*, you learn to relax the body mentally and physically to become non-resistant. You consciously relax all the muscles in your body and go with the fall. The impact with a relaxed fall is much softer than if your body is completely tensed up. And your ability to expel air from the lungs as you land spreads and distributes the force of the fall, thus protecting the body somewhat.

This relaxation might explain why intoxicated drivers walk away from an accident injury free, while sober drivers and/or passengers tend to be more badly injured. The drunk person's body is completely relaxed, both mentally and physically. The unlucky sober person's instinct is to tense their body, thus causing more harm upon impact. Hence, knowing how to relax during a fall and not use your hands or wrists to break it greatly reduces the risk of injury. These drills are practiced and repeated time and time again until relaxing when falling becomes second nature.

It takes weeks, months, years, even a lifetime to refine specific moves and techniques. I was going to learn to fall like a pro. For an entire month, I worked on the first step in not hurting myself—don't resist the fall.

After a few months, I advanced to some basic grabs and throws, but what I practiced those first few weeks applied to everything else I learned in martial arts. As Reed Sensei said, learning to punch and kick would come as I continued to advance in judo and karate. Practicing patience in everyday situations moving forward was going to be easy compared to physically falling night after night.

Have you ever been so driven and ambitious that the mere idea of waiting for the things you are pursuing feels utterly tortuous? Rest assured, you're not alone. But the road to mastering any art or enhancing any talent is paved with dedicated effort, often over a long period. Patience transforms relationships, helps you become empathetic, instills a positive attitude, and can make you healthier. It gives you a deeper appreciation and helps you suspend judgment long enough to make informed decisions, thus cutting a path to a happier, more successful, and more peaceful life with fewer regrets. So, relax and enjoy your journey.

MENTOR/MENTEE

Oprah Winfrey, best known for *The Oprah Winfrey Show*, was mentored by the celebrated author and poet, the late Maya Angelou. Angelou helped guide Winfrey through many obstacles throughout her life, including how to stay the course for her dreams and the importance of putting in the time required to achieve great success. Winfrey once said, "Mentors are important, and I don't think anybody makes it in the world without some form of mentorship."

She credits Angelou for always being there and for being a close friend.

SUMMARY

Learning to fall taught me the obvious lesson of how to protect my body and avoid injury, but the underlying lesson was that patience needs time to be cultivated and nurtured. There is no quick and easy way. Instant gratification will come and go and is of no intrinsic value. Patience is a state of being that occurs between experience and reaction. Whether you are trying to be patient with yourself, your children, employees, coworkers, management, or even the car driving in front of you that just cut you off, the ability to successfully deal with delays or obstacles takes patience. Practicing patience takes time, understanding, and a lifelong commitment.

The road to achievement can be very long, winding, and sometimes, mentally and physically strenuous. When you want things to happen, the wait is inevitable. Everything doesn't have to be learned or mastered in one session. How you deal with waiting and how you perceive that time is the most important factor. A journey requires patience, so those who want immediate results are sure to experience a long, uphill battle. Acting with patience is a way of telling life and the obstacles in front of you that you're in charge!

ACTION STEPS

THINK

Think about the last time you were impatient. What caused it? What did you do about it?

_____

_____

Name two things you have started and quit or not seen through because the end was not in sight.

_____

_____

Now, list two things you are most proud of seeing through to the end by being patient.

_____

_____

DO

Rushing and being impatient only waste time and energy. Slow down and take the necessary steps to move your life and career forward. Your ability to learn and retain things better and faster is prudent when determining your success and potential for personal growth.

Even when accelerating your learning curve, acquiring life and career skills is more effective if it is spread out, versus jamming it into a single class or lesson. It is okay to take a moment and formalize a timeline for the goals you set and wish to achieve.

Commit to a single goal, end result, or course of action that you are willing to do the work required for over a specific time period.

Then follow the schedule and timeline until your goal is achieved before quitting or moving on to the next one. Learn to fall correctly in everything you do before moving on to the more advanced or cooler things.

ND. # THE SUM OF 4

MENTOR • DEVELOP • EXECUTE • SUCCEED

CHAPTER 4
BUILDING A STRONG FOUNDATION

"To succeed, you will soon learn, as I did, the importance of a solid foundation in the basics of education—literacy, both verbal and numerical, and communication skills."

— Alan Greenspan

In the last chapter, I emphasized the importance of staying the course, doing the hard work required, and trusting the pace and flow, even when it seems impossible, to successfully master patience. In a nutshell, it's imperative to be more patient and understanding, delay gratification, and make a real effort to see things through to the end.

As I mentioned earlier, in the martial arts, you learn the basics, like how to properly form a fist and other simple techniques before learning the fancier, cinematic moves. As you progress through advanced levels of training, though, you're introduced to more effective, quicker, and more complicated moves and strikes. At that point, something fascinating happens. Instead of fully mastering something, you start over, only now with an arsenal of sound skills to build upon. The point from which you start over, after grasping the basics, is what's most important to grow and improve upon.

This chapter will delve into how learning the fundamentals helps you create a strong foundation. Whether it's investing, public speaking, writing code, learning a new language, or flying an airplane, appreciating the basics is essential. We'll discuss its value because everything you think, believe, and do is only as strong, effective, and successful as the foundation it's built on. A solid foundation ensures resilience against outside forces and guarantees one will never start over at zero. Without one, you set yourself up for failure, disaster, and often, pain. Do you remember *The Three Little Pigs*? Do you think the Big Bad Wolf would have had any chance against a pig that built the Great Pyramids? I certainly wouldn't waste my breath huffing and puffing away.

Let me ask you: Have you invested the time and effort to build a solid and successful foundation, equivalent to the Great Pyramids, in your life? Or have you haphazardly erected the tallest building you could in the shortest time possible? Are cracks beginning to appear in your foundation already? Basketball great Michael Jordan once said about the importance of building a strong foundation, "You can practice shooting eight hours a day, but if your technique is wrong, then all you become is very good at shooting the wrong way. Get the fundamentals down, and the level of everything you do will rise."

By learning and mastering the basic principles from the experts, you can easily avoid making unnecessary and costly mistakes. If your foundation is weak, then future challenges and any added weight will be harder to overcome and surely cause something to crack, break, or fall hard. Whereas, by investing the time to build a solid base and foundation, you will undoubtedly avoid these kinds of pitfalls, be more effective, less wasteful, and successfully handle multiple challenges simultaneously. Having sound experience and expert skills is a direct result of having a strong foundation.

The higher the building, the stronger the foundation needs to be. It is that simple. Each fall you experience helps build upon the foundation so it's even stronger the next time and better prepares you to avoid a fall in the future. Once you know how to fall correctly, you are prepared for the unknown because the foundation is secure, safe, easy to improve, and you can increase your building's height under all kinds of conditions. The life experiences and skills you develop are the bricks you build your life on after learning to fall efficiently. Once you have a sound foundation, you can easily adapt, change, and maneuver bricks to build the structure of your dreams.

Reed Sensei understood a person's strength lies in the foundation that keeps them upright and able to maintain their effectiveness. He sometimes sounded like a broken record when he pounded this motto into his students, "Building a strong foundation takes time and patience. The boring work must be done again and again and again. It is a process that isn't easy. And when you think you're done, you need to do it again. This applies to anything and everything, not just a basic karate stance."

As he so adamantly repeated, your foundation is the starting point for everything you do, including everything you wish to achieve, create, and enjoy. The more ambitious the goal, no matter in which area of life, the stronger your foundation must be. A skyscraper can't have the same foundation as a one-story building. Whether you're building a skyscraper, a fast food restaurant, or your resume, you need to put in the time necessary to lay the foundation required to achieve your desired success.

ONE BRICK AT A TIME

In his book *Outliers*, bestselling author Malcolm Gladwell shares the 10,000-hour rule, which states the key to achieving world-class expertise in *any* skill is practicing it correctly for at least 10,000 hours. This is not to be confused with my 10,000-knuckle push-up nightmare, by the way.

Bruce Lee said of the importance of practicing something and perfecting that single thing, "I fear not the man who has practiced 10,000 kicks once, but I fear the man who has practiced one kick 10,000 times."

I think what Malcolm Gladwell and Bruce Lee both were saying was that discipline and consistent practice, over and over again, are how you make your best better. Repetition makes you a master!

At age eight on my first day of class, I believed that by just showing up and walking in, somehow, I'd instantly become an expert martial artist. Instead, to my surprise, I spent the entire class and the next month learning to fall until my body was black and blue. All this time and bruising was used to gain a single basic skill that would lay the foundation of my martial arts journey.

Not everyone wants to become an *overnight ninja*, but most of us wish for skills, knowledge, power, and success without taking the risk, time, or necessary steps. I'm still guilty of desiring instant gratification and wanting a quick result without following the proper process. I wish to become instantly rich—take a magic pill to become CEO of a Fortune 500 company, eat Oreos and still have an eight-pack stomach, have the flexibility of Gumby, speak five languages, be a *New York Times* bestselling author, and be the best husband, dad, friend, and mentor.

These wants are certainly "Anything and everything in life." What they all have in common, besides being my own personal goals, is they are all fathomable, attainable, and possible. But none of them will come to fruition overnight. They all will take some sort of process, a starting point, sacrifice, and plenty of effort. Even connecting with someone who knows how to get there or has gotten there before is only a shortcut. Hard work and time are still requisites!

The effort must be made, floor by floor, to build a skyscraper. There's no "Penthouse with a view," without a sound foundation and solid floors to support it, built one brick at a time.

START BUILDING NOW

We all have personal goals, something we have always wanted to do, a place to see, or something to accomplish. Wishing to have started sooner in life, when we had more money or free time, is a common excuse. But the truth is it's never too late; we can accomplish any of those things still, today, right now. We simply must make the choice to start, just as the Chinese proverb says, "The best time to plant a tree was twenty years ago. The second-best time is now."

I don't remember the first time I heard that proverb, but it has always inspired me to be proactive with the choices I make. In my opinion, and many experts agree, the mere act of starting something is the most difficult part. It's hard to begin anything and extremely hard to set a strong foundation. If it were easy, everyone would be a black belt, a professional athlete, speak dozens of languages, sing like Justin Timberlake, be a billionaire like Bill Gates, or have more gold medals than Michael Phelps.

Hoping to have overnight success isn't a strategy—it's a pipe dream. The people mentioned above first learned from experts in their fields and then invested the time and effort necessary to create an unbreakable foundation. Once they decided to start, they mastered the fundamentals, and only then moved on to becoming phenomenal success stories. This is the winning strategy that brings success, but it comes only after years of hard work. If you go too fast, without a proper foundation, your building might crumble, sending you many steps backward. One step forward and two steps back isn't a winning strategy or conducive to achieving results or success.

If you've worked at something for many years, you may already have the experience and a well-set foundation; if not, you'll have to start with the basics. To become an expert and develop a specific skill or skills, use a step-by-step process, regardless of your starting point. Whether it's creating an everlasting bond with someone like your child, becoming a top salesperson, running your first marathon, graduating college, or being a group leader, you will first have to set up your foundation solidly, step by step.

DEALING WITH CRACKS

How good are you at *blank*? Sometimes you know, and sometimes, you don't. Sometimes you think you are better than you are. When you evaluate yourself, it can be difficult to see the big picture. You're so focused on yourself or your next move that it's hard to see yourself in the long-term. Being told you have cracks in your foundation can be a roundhouse kick to the ego. A mentor's fresh point of view, however, can be the secret ingredient to reinforce that weak point and turn it into a strength.

As a mentor, Reed Sensei had no problem identifying weaknesses in anyone's foundation. If he saw one, he wouldn't pull any punches. He could take a simple punch, explain its purpose and function, and then create a way for the student to build or reinforce their foundation to ensure they could deliver a devastating blow. American essayist, poet, and philosopher Henry David Thoreau once wrote, "If you have built castles in the air, your work need not be lost; that is where they should be. Now put the foundations under them."

This point was driven home one evening during karate class when we were practicing punching in place in front of the mirrors, looking at our own reflections. Over and over we punched, attempting to visualize an opponent. Our minds began to wander as the repetitions became repetitious—we were bored. Reed Sensei saw us mindlessly punching at ourselves, half-heartedly, with no true intent or power in our punches. Our sloppy, haphazard punching frustrated him enough that he let out a loud order to stop immediately.

When this man said, "Jump!" we all asked, "How high?" He was instrumental in starting and continually rewriting the Survival School handbook at Fairchild Airforce Base until retiring in 1971 from the USAF, a Korean and Vietnam War veteran. He was a close quarter combat tactician, eighth-degree black belt in both judo and Shotokan karate, on the first US Judo Olympic team as an alternate, a national and international judo champion, and belonged to the US Martial Arts Hall of Fame. He wasn't to be trifled with, and he could be ornery like a big bad bull who had horns—long, gnarly ones that none of us wanted to mess with!

After shouting, "Stop!", Reed Sensei walked to his desk and grabbed a marker. Then he ambled like a rhinoceros toward the mirror in the middle of the room. With the black permanent marker, he wrote the number 850 in the top left corner of the mirror. We were all concerned about the meaning of the random number, because nothing this man did was random; therefore, it couldn't be good. Since Spokane's area code was 509, I knew he wasn't giving us his phone number.

Everyone anxiously awaited the reason behind the numbers he had just written. A moment later, he informed us it was the number of push-ups we would do each class. Did this man just say *each* class, or did he mean just for tonight? He clarified by saying, "I don't expect everyone to do all of them non-stop, but we are all doing them until you get to that number before the end of class every night."

Even at age twelve, I truly pitied the students in the other classes, not privy to that night's infamous 850 description. That number stayed on that mirror for years! And I mean years—to the tune of at least twenty-five years! That's the kind of push-up practice we got seven days a week, sometimes twice a day. To the best of my knowledge, it was still there well after I went off to college, until Reed Sensei finally closed the dojo's doors just a few years ago.

Besides being a great workout, the physical challenge was meant to help us practice something so basic, so many times, that we could do it automatically. We not only became stronger, but we learned to become proficient at pushing and pulling. It was like the quote from Bruce Lee above about practicing one thing 10,000 times. To save you time figuring it out, we did just over 300,000 push-ups a year. I'm too afraid to take that number and multiply it by twenty-five, but I will attribute my competition wins and confidence in my punches to whatever that number is.

BUILDING A STRONG FOUNDATION

Reed Sensei had noticed our weak pull and extension on punches. He saw we had major cracks in our foundations that needed immediate repair. That night, we needed to refocus and reset our minds. It was time to stop, assess, adjust, and then implement to improve our punching foundation.

Remember, there's no fast track or secret magical pill to accomplishing something or becoming proficient at it. By setting strong foundations, you are fortifying yourself against future or current problems that may impede, slow, or prevent you from building your beautiful building and reaching your goal. It's also important to caution that even after setting a strong foundation, new challenges will always arise, with new obstacles, setbacks, distractions, technologies, or ways to do something that require you to stop, assess, adjust, and implement in a stronger way.

None of us are immune to setbacks. Setbacks teach and remind you to continuously strive to improve and move forward, whereas taking steps back is usually avoidable and the result of being too hasty, ill prepared, or having an inadequate foundation.

Stop to assess how strong your foundation is. Is it made of straw or bricks? If there are flaws, it's time to revisit the basics. A better understanding of the fundamentals is necessary to improving or becoming an expert at something. Now's not the time to wait. It's time to begin—start right now!

MENTOR/MENTEE

Warren Buffett, the Berkshire Hathaway CEO often considered the most successful investor in history, mentored Microsoft cofounder Bill Gates. Gates credited Buffett with teaching him to deal with difficult situations and to think long-term. Currently, as one of the richest people in the world, Gates greatly admires Buffett's life and ability to make complex things easy for everyone to understand. Gates also commends Buffett's belief in having a strong foundation to build and grow upon. In addition, both Buffett and Gates, over the years, have felt empowered by each other.

SUMMARY

The key lesson is rather straightforward—your foundation matters! Whether it's in your health and fitness, relationships, finances, or any other area. Before achieving success, you must first have a solid foundation to build upon. Whoever coined the phrase "Time is money" probably knew from experience the cost of making mistakes and starting over from scratch.

Foundation building shouldn't be done hastily. Taking the time to lay the groundwork correctly requires time and effort. And your work is never really finished until your last breath is spent. There will always be room for improvement. Reevaluate on a regular basis. Problems should be tackled immediately to ensure efficiency.

Knowing your fundamentals are sound and that your foundation is solid will guarantee success in any situation or environment and your confidence will radiate. Remember, if you start to feel like your skyscraper is shaking, climb down, look at your foundation, and if necessary, strengthen it. Don't let your life collapse due to impatience or by being too slow to solidify your foundation. Don't be afraid to progress slowly, but always be very afraid to stop.

ACTION STEPS

THINK

What are you doing daily to create better foundations in all aspects of your life?

_____

_____

_____

Write three skills or achievements you would like to attain.

1. _____
2. _____
3. _____

Whom do you know with expertise, experience, or knowledge about these skills or achievements you wish to attain whom you could recruit?

_____

_____

_____

Now write the steps and realistic timelines for achieving these goals.

_____

78 THE SUM OF 4

_____

_____

DO

Inspect your foundation regularly. Stop, assess, adapt, adjust, and then implement your improvements immediately!

Whatever you want to achieve or learn, find the basic framework, system, or principle, and master it.

When you do face a setback, learn from it and keep moving forward!

PART II
DEVELOP

THE SUM OF 4

MENTOR · **DEVELOP** · EXECUTE · SUCCEED

CHAPTER 5
ENCOURAGING RESPECT

"Treat people the way you want to be treated.
Talk to people the way you want to be talked to.
Respect is earned, not given."

— Hussein Nishah

So far, I have stressed the importance of practicing patience and securing a solid base in pursuit of your goals, reassessing for faults, and repairing before significant damage occurs. It's imperative to do things one step at a time, which can sometimes be an extremely long process. By surrounding ourselves with mentors or outside points of view, it becomes easier to detect, solve, and patch holes in our daily lives. A great mentor will remind you to stay focused, explain how to avoid costly mistakes, bring weaknesses and faults to your attention through constructive criticism, point out strengths, and advise you in how to improve yourself to achieve greater success.

In this chapter, I'll highlight the most effective and natural way to get the results you want. There's no easy path to developing it or applying this simple and timeless formula, but if you can, there is no purer way to build your success in your personal and career life. The answer is so obvious that we tend to forget it, overlook it, or brush it off rather than work harder at using its power. The formula is simple, really. It is about having respect and a true link between two parties. It's about earning the respect of others and developing the self-respect to know your own value and worthiness. It's also about using empathy and kindness to treat people fairly, the way they need and deserve to be treated.

Who would you do anything for—not because you must but because you want to? Is there someone who would do anything for you? Think of all the different situations and relationships you've had throughout your life and the countless opportunities to interact with people, family, employees, colleagues, corporate leaders, high-ranking officials, or anyone you've come across. Who, of all these people you know or have met, do you desire to be more like or wish to emulate? These are the people you are most likely to be loyal to and respect. Those we respect the most motivate us to go places we would never otherwise go.

THE GOLDEN RULE

Matthew 7:12: "So in everything, do unto others what you would have them do to you." This Bible verse and the great Chinese philosopher, Confucius, share a similar maxim echoed by religious leader, Rabbi Hillel, who said, "Do not do to others what you would not want others to do to you."

Both verses issue similar injunctions that are among the highest and most beautiful things philosophy and religion have to offer. Either verse lays out the most basic way to earn respect: to treat others the way you would like to be treated. Respect is built over time, and it is only achieved when others trust you.

WHAT IS RESPECT?

Respect is taking someone else's needs, feelings, ideas, and thoughts into consideration. When interacting with them, you take their position into account. It also means treating yourself and other people, places, and things as if they are special. And finally, it means admiring others and honoring their wishes, background, and knowledge even when it's different than your own.

We all want and sometimes demand respect from others. Or at the minimum, we want them to understand our point of view. There's no law that says you must like everyone or respect everyone, but there's a growing need for us all to be able to put ourselves in others' shoes and walk their walk before judging them. We want our kids, peers, colleagues, and significant others to respect us. And the truth is they all want our respect as well. So, who respects who first, or does it matter? It's kind of like asking, "Which came first, the chicken or the egg?"

What matters is that we start by respecting ourselves and becoming more aware of how we treat other people. This will ensure we are giving each person the respect they are entitled to as a fellow human being. Your actions and words are a representation of yourself. Learning to respect others will help you respect yourself, and then you will be able to treat yourself as well as others with greater dignity and consideration. This attitude will put you one step closer to learning how to fully love yourself and everyone else. Irish novelist Laurence Sterne said it best when connecting self-respect to the value of respecting others, "Respect for ourselves guides our morals; respect for others guides our manners."

ADMIRATION

Let's look at some of the people we admire. It may be the well-dressed tailor, a successful small business owner who started out of their garage, an Olympic athlete for their athletic ability, a teacher who influenced you in some way, a parent who puts in the time and sacrifice to be a great parent, or a dentist for their knowledge of your teeth. What's the common theme?

After careful thought, we see that what we respect and admire is their discipline. We wouldn't respect a sloppy tailor. We wouldn't respect a small business owner who stole from their employees. We wouldn't respect an Olympic athlete who uses performance-enhancing substances. Nor a dentist with missing teeth. Hence, what we tend to admire, respect, and emulate in others is their discipline.

The way we act, our own discipline, and paying attention to helping others as they develop their skills and knowledge, is what earns us respect. Being respected by people we respect and admire throughout our lives teaches us how to be respectful toward others. It's a two-way street that builds feelings of trust, security, and wellbeing.

Putting this into practice is the hard part. There's no shortage of forces in our society and culture that ignore the value of respect. Whether it's someone rolling their eyes, doing an outrageous dance in the face of the losing team, not shaking hands with the winning team, or humiliating someone over social media, making our society more respectful can sometimes be daunting and feel like an uphill battle.

The need for mutual respect absolutely applies to our corporate workforce as well as our personal lives. This is a fight worth fighting for the sake of our relationships with our kids, students, leaders, employees, and colleagues. This isn't a losing battle, but a challenge that takes effort, and it begins with and requires mutual respect.

Schools, sports, businesses, and faith communities, for example, aim to instill values like respect, but like most child education, respect begins at home. Take, for example, the thank you note for someone's time or advice. My mom taught me that uttering a simple "thank you" not only makes someone feel appreciated, but it could also open many future doors for me. A sincere thank you meant you were humble and appreciative, and it could make or break the tone of a relationship. Although I agreed with my dad that a handshake is very important when meeting someone, a firm handshake doesn't guarantee you know anything about someone's true character.

BOW...WOW...WOW

Reed Sensei was very humble and respectful, while still confident. How? Through eye contact, body language, and a simple bow.

The bow is an extremely important feature of Japanese etiquette—so much so that, although children normally learn to bow at a very young age, Japanese companies and martial arts dojos provide training to their employees and students in how to bow correctly. There are three types of bows: informal, formal, and extremely formal. The etiquette surrounding bowing, including the length, depth, and appropriate response is exceedingly complex, but for simplicity's sake, understand that a bow is much more than a simple greeting. It can convey emotions, such as appreciation, remorsefulness, and most importantly, respect.

Early in my judo and karate training, not only did we work on the basics of self-defense, but we invested time to learn to bow and the meaning behind its importance. Typically, before sparring in karate, judo, or kendo, both opponents bow to their judge or referee, and then face one another to bow again. I vividly remember the excitement I felt one night at finally sparring, practicing my newly acquired, non-ninja skills.

I hastily bowed to Reed Sensei and then quickly turned to bow to my opponent. But before I could even finish my halfhearted bow, I felt the grip of a pit bull's bite at the nape of my neck. I looked like a baby kitten being carried away, hanging three inches off the ground in its mother's jaws.

Reed Sensei pulled me off the mat and literally carried me away from the rest of the class, placing me in the corner of the room like "Baby" in the movie *Dirty Dancing*. Not knowing the cause of my hover board ride and standing in utter shock, I listened to him as he quietly lectured me on the importance of a bow.

"Blue," he said, "respect is one of the cornerstone skills in life you must possess, and self-respect is the one thing we can control. Caring about yourself, your efforts, thoughts, self-discipline, and the way people perceive you is imperative in this world. Give a damn about how people see you! Don't think about yourself in a conceited or narcissistic way, but as a person who can be trusted and is reliable, loyal, caring, and genuine. Bowing makes you vulnerable to the person in front of you. It's not the physical bow, but rather the intent behind it. It opens you up and lays it all out for everyone to see. Showing you have nothing to hide or gain. It's mutual respect in the rawest form between you and another person."

Embarrassed, and with tears swelling in my eyes, I accepted that

I had just been schooled on the importance of training with good etiquette. Deep down, however, I had just been reminded that if you don't respect yourself, maintain discipline, and respect others, you cannot expect to earn the respect of another.

Everyone knows someone with bad manners, someone who lacks respect or acts in a disrespectful way. Picture this person in your mind. Now, think about what their life is like. Are they successful in all aspects of their life? Do you or other people gravitate toward them? Do they have respect from others? If you said *no* to any of these questions, it's possible they probably have fewer true friends and lack others' trust.

On the other hand, someone like the late philanthropist and President of South Africa, Nelson Mandela, who was kind, humble, disciplined, and had great self-respect for himself and his fellow South Africans, could seamlessly blend and integrate into different groups and environments. Who wants to support, associate with, or work for someone they don't respect, who is selfish, and/or who acts like a mean ogre?

The effect our behavior has on our students, friends, employees, bosses, and our family is greater than any of us can measure. The type of effect, positive or negative, depends on the ability to maintain this two-way street of mutual respect. It should be our aim, as parents, friends, mentors, teachers, or leaders, to choose to live this way and to instill these values in those who surround us. Just like author Roy T. Bennett said, "Even if you cannot change all the people around you, you can change the people you choose to be around. Life is too short to waste your time on people who don't respect, appreciate, and value you. Spend your life with people who make you smile, laugh, and feel loved."

R.E.L.A.T.E.

Again, I ask who would you do anything for without expecting anything in return? Is it because they treat you the way you want to be treated, or maybe, the way you need to be treated? Is this feeling reciprocated, and if not, would you be okay with that? Out of everyone you've ever met, who would you do this for because you want to, not because you were required to? The handful of people who come to mind are the ones you Respect, wish to Emulate, Love, Admire, Trust, and are Empathetic to the most. A simple way to remember those we are most willing to look up to and aspire to be like is with the acronym R.E.L.A.T.E. These are not only the people you should surround yourself with, but like Reed Sensei did with me, they have the power to bring out your full potential!

Remember, just being in the proximity of successful people and high achievers doesn't guarantee you will become successful yourself. The relationship and connection must have some combination or all parts of R.E.L.A.T.E. to perform at a truly higher level you didn't know you could. In return, R.E.L.A.T.E. serves as the secret catalyst that ignites or initiates the spark and driving force behind compressing decades of experience and knowledge into months or days.

MENTOR/MENTEE

Oscar-winning actor Denzel Washington always admired and respected actor Sidney Poitier. Denzel has often referred to Poitier as his mentor and credits Poitier's own acting career and life as instrumental to his own career. Emulating and following Poitier's sage advice over the years—they were great friends—helped Washington evolve into one of the most successful and well-paid actors.

SUMMARY

Gaining the respect of others is no easy task, but it is the most effective way to become a strong, influential, and great leader. Treating others with respect is a timeless method for respecting yourself. Those we respect bring out the best in us because we want to emulate them. We admire and want to mimic their discipline. Surrounding ourselves with those we respect and admire, as in R.E.L.A.T.E., is the most powerful way to tap into our best selves and shorten our learning curve. These are the people for whom we would do 10,000 push-ups.

When you show respect, you encourage caring relationships and foster their positive development. Even though Reed Sensei pulled me off the mat that day, he successfully imparted the importance and value of being respectful to others as a form of self-respect. This lecture not only publicly shamed and embarrassed me, but taught me that self-respect is learned, and without it, no one will respect you.

ACTION STEPS

THINK

Write down the names of at least two people who easily fit the R.E.L.A.T.E. model.

_____

_____

92   THE SUM OF 4

List why you respect certain people and not others.

_____

_____

In what ways could these people get or regain your respect?

_____

_____

What can you do to earn the respect of others such as your colleagues, bosses, family, and friends?

_____

_____

_____

_____

DO

Respect yourself first. Know your worth and value. Be proud of you!

Become more observant about other people's feelings and lives. Treat everyone you meet the way you'd like to be treated. Practice thinking from other people's points of view; put yourself in their shoes, and truly listen to their values.

Surround yourself with those you wish to be friends with, who support you and bring you up. Those you Respect, wish to Emulate,

Love, Admire, Trust, and are most Empathetic toward.

Although connections and relationships to mentors, leaders, influencers, or others who can help you get the results you want are important, having a true connection with them through the R.E.L.A.T.E. combination is the secret to guaranteeing you reach your goals and turn them into reality faster.

THE SUM OF 4

MENTOR • **DEVELOP** • EXECUTE • SUCCEED

CHAPTER 6
CREATING AN EMOTIONAL CONNECTION

> "I've learned that people will forget what you said, people will forget what you did, but people will never forget how you made them feel."
>
> — Maya Angelou

In the last chapter, we defined respect and the importance of self-respect. We also discussed how surrounding yourself with and committing to modeling someone you connect or R.E.L.A.T.E. with is the ultimate way to get the results you dream about. We must also take an honest look at ourselves and how we treat the people around us. This analysis comes before we can become respect worthy. The best way to earn respect is to understand that respect is a direct reflection of how you listen to others and follow the Golden Rule.

As I mentioned earlier, various tried and true ways exist to earn respect. I have come to believe a strong correlation also exists between the respect we have for people and the bond we have with them. Those we have the greatest respect and admiration for are the people with whom we feel the strongest emotional connection and have the best relationships.

Think back to a time you didn't get picked for a team, or felt excluded or left behind. Or a time you had nothing in common with anyone in the room, at work, at a party, or at a job interview. Did this feeling of disconnect motivate or demotivate you? On the flipside, how important and valued do you feel when someone pays attention to you, puts you first, includes you, or intently listens and engages with you? This sense of belonging and being valued by those around you is priceless.

Obviously, we feel differently about someone we feel connected to. The ability to successfully relate to others is what creates a strong emotional connection. A nexus of one person to another, coupled with the sense of belonging, determines the strength of a relationship. It creates an environment that supports mutual respect, involvement, engagement, loyalty, advocacy, and trust. Research professor, TED talk speaker, and *New York Times* bestselling author Brené Brown defines the human connection as, "The energy that exists between people when they feel seen, heard, and valued; when they can give and receive without judgment; and when they derive sustenance and strength from the relationship."

In other words, when one unfailingly engages with someone else, puts the other first, and makes them feel important and included, it is the surest way to create loyalty and a strong connection with that person. This link brings together followers and leaders in mutual respect. The sense of belonging to those around us, ultimately, improves our wellbeing.

Authentically connecting to someone is a learned skill that takes time and effort but can produce amazing results. In fact, Theo Epstein, the president of baseball operations with the Chicago Cubs, credits his team's World Series Championship to the players' connection, saying, "When people do things they weren't even sure they were capable of, I think it comes back to connection. Connection with teammates. Connection with the organization. Feeling like they belong in the environment. I think it's a human need—the need to feel connected. We don't live in isolation. Most people don't like working in isolation—some do, but typically, they don't end up playing Major League Baseball."

We have an innate desire to feel valued, important, respected, heard, and accepted by others. This is what a human or emotional connection is. To be truly successful at creating a personal connection with a team, coworker, manager, customer, or family member takes effort, sacrifice, and time because it requires earning the respect and trust of others. It's a two-way street, and if one side is congested or becomes blocked, the other side will, in turn, become ineffective.

THE SUM OF 4

Take a moment to think about how you would give directions to Disneyland in California? You might use the quickest or least expensive route. Perhaps it might be more scenic or one with your favorite restaurants. Your steps and instructions could, and probably would, vary extremely from someone else's. Depending on the date or even the moment you enter a location or destination, the map or mobile app you use could result in numerous paths, taking into consideration high traffic times, road construction, or other variables. In math and psychology, this phenomenon is known as equifinality. Equifinality basically states that the same end state or result can be achieved via many different means, paths, or trajectories.

I happened to realize and experience equifinality firsthand while learning the correct way to deliver and finish a front kick with maximum power and smoothness. After delivering a kick, I immediately would land with a loud thud. Reed Sensei, as well as many other instructors, would respond with instructions for me to land "softer" or "like a butterfly." For years and well into my martial art training, no matter what anyone advised or instructed, nothing they said resonated with me, and I still sounded like an elephant's stomp.

Finally, a younger instructor pulled me aside and used a simple and primitive analogy to find a way for me to land with more finesse. He said, "Imagine you are a sunny side up egg and your arms and legs are the yolk. The yolk is malleable, elastic, and can move in any direction. Whereas your stationary leg and body are the egg white, which is solid and never moves."

The result was immediate! I didn't land like a sack of potatoes each and every kick I delivered from that point on. This was my aha moment. By finding a different way or formula, someone had successfully unlocked a door in my brain that no one else had been able to. This pivotal moment is what led me to developing and formulating a system to efficiently and successfully reach and resonate with so many others.

Quickly think about an equation that gets to the sum of 4. I would get to 4 with the equation $2 + 2$, but for you, it might be $1 + 3$. Both equal 4 and get to the same answer, but the path we followed is different. The actual number 4, or any other number for that matter, isn't the point. The most important part is realizing there are numerous and no right or wrong ways to any destination, goal, or dream.

Every way has its advantages and disadvantages. Understanding that no two people learn, think, communicate, interpret, process, or do things the same way is imperative to being an effective listener and communicator. This helps explain why some leaders, parents, mentors, and teachers are able to inspire, motivate, and reach people so effectively, when others are not.

We all can create a path to a certain destination, but very few of us know how someone else gets to that destination. As a result, most of us tend to answer, teach, communicate, or process one-sidedly. We think our way is the best or only way to do something. However, the most inspiring, motivating, and effective people think outside the box. They discover and observe how others think, what resonates for them, or how they enjoy reaching their sum of 4.

This is the ultimate key to unlocking the door and bridging the gap to those around you. When giving a speech, selling, promoting, training, teaching, or speaking to your child, if either party doesn't understand how the other gets to their number or what their learning style is, the message may become mixed or misunderstood. To effectively communicate and create a strong connection, one or both sides must understand how each gets to their sum of 4. Otherwise, a disconnect exists that makes the message undeliverable.

Learning to effectively listen and communicate with everyone we encounter will create an effective path for connecting with them. The ability to connect builds the trust and respect required to communicate effectively and lead powerfully. Author, philanthropist, and management consultant Peter Drucker once said, "The most important thing in communication is hearing what isn't said."

PATERNAL DISCONNECT

Connecting with Reed Sensei was as easy as getting butter to melt on top of a hot waffle because he paid attention to me, listened well, and made me feel valued and important. He effortlessly became a father figure to me because our connection and relationship was organic.

Unfortunately, around the time I turned ten, my parents divorced. Then my connection with my dad began to crumble. Like many young boys, I realized my father and I had less and less in common. My relationship with my dad slowly became distant and less involved until communicating with him was like trying to get blood out of a turnip.

In retrospect, I know it wasn't because he didn't love me or want me to have a wonderful life; he was just absent. Simply put, he didn't know how to be a successful father. As a result, my respect for my father began to wane, and we began to lose our emotional connection, making it difficult to communicate effectively for nearly thirty years, until right before he passed away.

BREAKFAST WITH DARTH VADER

Eating together was never a tradition for my family. That is, unless you call eating around the television with lap trays, while watching *60 Minutes* or Steven Spielberg's *Amazing Stories* on Sunday nights a tradition. Other than holidays, a Saturday breakfast was usually the only meal we enjoyed together.

I will credit my mom's popular 2,000-plus calorie breakfast for bringing us together most Saturdays. My favorite was the lightly crisp, extra fatty, bacon-filled waffles I'd cover with real butter and drown with sugar-packed syrup. Mom would add eraser-size chunks of bacon into the batter before pouring it into a dented steel waffle maker that weighed at least five pounds. I guarantee, the leftover residue from the previous waffle breakfast added to its weight.

She would say of the old residue, "Makes it taste better." I never believed that for a minute. Don't even get me started about the heavy black cast iron skillet she kept in the oven that was filled with old bacon grease from who knows when. You know, the kind of skillet you're not supposed to clean because it's bad for the pan's lifespan? Yuck! What about my lifespan? Cleaning it with soap and leaving a two-inch thick layer of Crisco and old bacon grease are two different things. Sanitary or not, because of that waffle maker, Eggo waffles never have been my favorite.

My dad had eating his breakfast down to a science, which I loved to try to mimic. He never veered from his process. With his right hand, he would consume three super-runny, sunny-side-up eggs, one piece of toasted white Wonder Bread, and one waffle with syrup. If there were hash browns, he'd mix them into carb madness on his plate. I wouldn't be doing this description justice if I omitted my least favorite part of his routine, one I never copied, which was to smoke five to seven Marlboro cigarettes throughout breakfast.

My dad used his left hand solely to hold Spokane's local newspaper, which, once opened, held his complete attention—the stove could have blown up and he'd still be reading. This was when I first noticed his wants took precedence, and his ability to relate and communicate with me began to deteriorate. One morning, I tried explaining how one of our three German Shepherds, currently under the dining table waiting for bacon scraps to drop, had just brutally dismembered my favorite G.I. Joe ninja action figure, Storm Shadow. My dad didn't so much as lift his eyes from the article he was reading.

Losing your favorite toy to the clenches of a canine's jaws was a huge deal for a nine-year-old. No medic, super glue, or arts and crafts skills could bring my poor Cobra ninja back to life. I was so devastated because he was one of the rarest figures to have in 1984. In the world of G.I. Joe, I couldn't imagine Cobra defeating, "The Real American Hero" without the assistance of this key player. It would be like the LA Lakers playing an entire season without the help of LeBron James. Just ludicrous.

Life as I knew it couldn't go on without immediately replacing Storm Shadow. I didn't just *want* a new G.I. Joe; I *needed* a new one! Explaining in detail to my dad the importance of replacing this action figure was useless. Not getting the reaction I was looking for, I simply asked for a ride to the local Toys "R" Us to use my own money for a replacement. Getting my dad to give me a ride there was one thing, finding this popular figure on the shelf would be another. I wasn't the only kid who loved G.I. Joe in the '80s, but I hoped Toys "R" Us' mascot Geoffrey the Giraffe wouldn't let me down.

Feeling I was speaking to a brick wall, I changed my begging tactics by simply yelling. "Please pay attention to me!" Without moving his eyes from the paper, my dad calmly responded, "I am, and I heard you. You want a new Darth Vader guy. I can do more than one thing at a time, by the way."

Was he serious? That didn't seem like successful multi-tasking to me since he thought I was asking for Darth Vader. There was nothing wrong with the Sith Lord; he was doing just fine resting in his own personal action figure carrying case, along with the rest of my *Star Wars* action figures. Unlike my G.I. Joe guy Storm Shadow, Lord Vader had successfully used his dark sorcery skills to avoid being consumed by one of our devil dogs.

My dad missed the boat that morning, or in this case, the Millennium Falcon. In case you are worried, many weeks later, I did get a new Storm Shadow. I just had to ask my mom for a ride instead and personally cover the cost of the new toy: $2.98 plus tax. Ouch. Today, Storm Shadow still stands proudly on my office shelf, right next to my uneaten Darth Vader.

A FATHER FIGURE

The most valuable tools a parent can have are to be present and to have real communication with their child. Every conversation with a child is important because it offers a plethora of information that can bring crucial things to the surface. Knowing your child better than they know themselves is invaluable. My dad never truly had that with me, but Reed Sensei successfully fulfilled it.

Because my dad was my father and would always be my father, my sensei chose to be my mentor and instructor. My father's role was different from a mentor's because it was permanent and mandatory. My dad responded to me out of necessity and authority, instead of common interests and understanding. By listening, engaging, and being present, my dad could have reconnected us successfully.

Instead, my relationship with Reed Sensei and the class became the new constant in my life. Martial arts became my discipline. My dedication to it caused my appreciation for it to grow each day. I was in class every chance I got because I loved being there and being around this man who had become not only a mentor, but a father figure to me.

Reed Sensei used martial arts as an expression of who he was and a symbol of what he believed. Because he took it very seriously, I took it seriously. If I hadn't, it would have looked like I wasn't taking him—a man whose values I respected—seriously. I believe my level of respect for him is why he took me under his wing and invested so much time and effort in me. Training established a nexus between us of shared passion, respect, and effective communication.

To this day, I wish my connection with my father had never been lost. When I was young, he was my idol, and I wanted to be just like him. As I grew older, however, as many fathers and sons do, we went our separate ways, losing the ability to relate to and communicate with each other.

Looking back at my relationship with my dad, especially after having a child of my own, reminds me a significant difference exists between being a father and a dad. Father is a proper term for a male who produces a child. But in a kid's eyes, a father is a dad. However, *dad* is a distinction that must be earned—just like that of great leader. Being considered a dad is earned by supporting your child financially and emotionally. Connecting with your children and genuinely being interested in them makes them feel important, valued, and respected. Be a good listener, be present, find common ground, encourage them, and try to relate to and understand them. You don't become a dad (or an effective mentor or leader) without working hard and being there when your child (or mentee or team) needs you.

How important is a sense of belonging, feeling valued, and heard by others to you? If these feelings aren't present, does it make you feel disrespected, undervalued, or left out? On the flipside, how do you feel when you're treated with respect, listened to, included, or made to feel important? Do these feelings motivate you and make you want to reciprocate and even go above and beyond for the person who treats you well?

Finding how we get to the sum of 4 and bringing out the best in us is the role an effective and successful leader, mentor, or parent plays. They attempt a different approach to get a different result, if what is currently being used isn't getting the results desired. They continually put effort in to connect and communicate with the people they interact with. This connection creates a bond among all parties involved and inspires everyone to perform at peak levels. It is the secret formula to reaching your followers, colleagues, children, sales-reps, employees, or whoever crosses your path.

Never lose the ability to connect and give another your full attention.

MENTOR/MENTEE

Director and producer J. J. Abrams first met Steven Spielberg at the age of sixteen. At that time, Spielberg had rediscovered old movies he thought he had lost, and he hired Abrams to help clean and salvage them. Since Abrams successfully saved the films, he and Spielberg had an absolute trust that developed between them, helping them become very close. They follow each other's careers to this day. In fact, many people consider Abrams the "new Spielberg."

SUMMARY

Making people feel appreciated, valued, respected, heard, and a part of something is the secret to successfully leading and connecting with people. Putting someone first and making them feel noticed or included is the surest way to gain their respect. A loyalty link or bond, a human connection, must be formed for any relationship to blossom. This connection can only happen if both parties are present in the moment. A relationship based on trust and respect will create a sense of belonging and improve your own wellbeing and the wellbeing of those around you.

A relationship is doomed without this link. To achieve an everlasting connection, you must listen as much as you talk. Give people a chance to reach out, be heard, and understood. This will unlock the door to the minds and hearts of those you meet. It will allow you to realize their sum of 4. Never stop talking and listening to those you interact with. Value and respect everyone you meet because the reward will outweigh the effort. People will naturally follow those who value and respect them. This, in turn, will bring out the best in them—and in you.

ACTION STEPS

THINK

How well connected do you feel to those you surround yourself with, either at work or at home?

_____

_____

CREATING AN EMOTIONAL CONNECTION 107

People learn in different ways, speak different languages, and do math differently. Do you communicate solely with one mode, or are you flexible with your communication style? How do you get to the sum of 4?

_____

_____

List several things you do every day to make others feel included, part of the group, important, and valued.

_____

_____

_____

_____

DO

Discover what makes others tick, what resonates with them, or how they get to their sum of 4.

Keep conversations from becoming a one-way street or dead end by being present when you engage with others. Remove distractions and be in the now. Value the time and connection for what it is.

Know who Darth Vader is and be able to distinguish his action figure from others.

Think of one positive thing to tell everyone around you. Tell them why you value, respect, and appreciate them.

Make others feel comfortable, included, and important, especially if you notice a disconnect.

Pay attention to those who reach out to you. Don't let their voices go unheard—you might hear something you need to know.

Put time and effort into creating a human and emotional connection with those you interact with. This small sacrifice may not only bring out the best in them, but the best in you.

THE SUM OF 4

MENTOR · **DEVELOP** · EXECUTE · SUCCEED

CHAPTER 7
LEARNING FROM BAD EXAMPLES

"I'm not totally useless. I can be used as a bad example."

— Victor Hugo, *Les Misérables*

The importance and benefit of a strong connection with another is undeniable. As a mentor or leader, there's no better way to naturally bring out the best in others than by creating a sense of belonging, acceptance, appreciation, importance, and personal value. This bond takes effort and time from both parties to earn mutual trust. Communication is a two-way street—make being present in the moment a priority and allow relationships to truly blossom.

Michelle Obama, Oprah Winfrey, and Mother Teresa are positive and influential examples of women who have lived successful, meaningful lives. Their paths show us how to elevate ourselves and achieve success through sincerely being in the moment, caring, and intentionally listening to others. In this chapter, however, we'll look at how a bad example can be just as revealing, valuable, and instructional as a good one. Sometimes the great lessons come from the worst examples.

Have you ever thought about why you are the way you are or why you make the decisions and choices you make? Maybe right now you're thinking of all the positive role models who have influenced you. Can you think of anything you may have learned from negative role models as well? Perhaps you look at people and scratch your head in amazement or disbelief, wondering how they have what they have or how they got where they are. You may know many people or leaders whom you don't admire and aspire to emulate because they set disappointing examples.

As disappointing as these negative role models may seem, they are useful, relevant, and good for us. Learning from them helps us avoid making their same mistakes. They are warning signs that keep us from driving off the road. We are all a mix of the good and bad examples we have witnessed, and we have strengths and weaknesses based on those experiences. Author, novelist, and poet Richelle E. Goodrich said it best, "From good examples, we learn how to be. From bad examples, we learn how not to be. An observant and willing student can learn from any circumstance."

By peering into the lives of those who have fallen before us, we can often discover the cause of their fall. If we see the cause, we can choose a different road, or at least travel on the same path in a different or more efficient way.

INDIANA JONES CHOSE WISELY

As a kid, The Indiana Jones trilogy was second only to *Star Wars* for me. I must have watched each of those movies at least one hundred times. I'm surprised the VHS tapes and our VCR lasted as long as they did. The last chapter of the trilogy, *Indiana Jones and the Last Crusade*, ends with Harrison Ford, who plays Indiana Jones, having to make a life or death choice. If you haven't seen these movies, shame on you; you deserve this spoiler.

In one of the last scenes, Indiana is given only one chance to correctly pick and drink from the Holy Grail (the true Cup of Christ) from an array of options. Choosing the correct cup will save his father, who is dying in an adjacent room, because the cup gives the gift of life. Indiana has seen others before him choose unwisely and instantly die. If he chooses the wrong cup, not only will he die, but so will his father. It is all or nothing. He must choose quickly because time has run out.

Of course, Indiana chooses wisely and saves himself and his father. Yes, he made a good choice, but first, he learned what cups not to choose from the people who died before he made his own choice. He learned from their mistakes.

THE CHOICE BELONGS TO YOU

Having choice is what it means to be alive. Some choices are easier than others, but circumstances and influences dictate the choices we make. Sometimes we make the right choices, and sometimes we make the wrong ones. I know firsthand because I've made some doozies. The point is we all have the ability, when given options, to make a choice. In some cases, it might feel like an ultimatum, or worse, that no options exist. Other times, it may seem like there are too many options, which can feel overwhelming and difficult.

You may not always like your options or position after you choose a certain path, but I assure you, you always have a choice! The outcome of that choice may have positive or negative consequences. For Indiana Jones, it was a life or death choice. Our choices may be simply how to save for retirement, ask for a raise or promotion, ask someone on a date, or even say no when offered drugs or alcohol.

The Dalai Lama said it best, "We can let the circumstances of our lives harden us so that we become increasingly resentful and afraid, or we can let them soften us and make us kinder. You always have the choice."

We are free to choose our path, but we must also own the results, taking responsibility for our choices. We all come from different backgrounds and were raised differently, but just because we grew up in a certain environment doesn't mean we will end up a certain way.

Obviously, we would all prefer a positive role model, manager, mentor, or leader. But if we can see a bad example in a different light, we can think of them as a good example instead—not because their behavior is good, but rather, because they help us isolate and understand their behaviors as undesirable and inefficient. This, in turn, helps make us aware of our own actions, choices, and behavior.

THE APPLE DOESN'T FALL FAR FROM THE TREE

The classic idiom "The apple doesn't fall far from the tree" refers to children who act like their parents. Negative learned behaviors often stem from childhood experiences. Children learn from their parents, so any positive or negative behaviors are likely to be passed on.

If you shook my family's apple tree, bottles would fall out. When my dad's drinking started to get out of hand, Reed Sensei saw the behavior could be a problem for my future. One morning after class, he basically asked how I was handling my parents' late-night parties. He didn't know how much I hated cleaning up cigarette butts most mornings, but he could certainly read the embarrassment and shame on my face.

Reed Sensei smiled slightly, and then he shared a parable with me that neatly captured the choice before me:

> Two brothers were raised in Reno, where their dad was a violent alcoholic and gambler. One brother grew up losing his paychecks at local casinos and drinking heavily, while the other brother never drank, became rich, and was a great dad. When asked how they came to be who they were, they gave the same answer, "Given who my dad was, how could I not?"

This parable can teach us two things: 1) No matter where you come from or who your influences are, you still control your own destiny; 2) We can always choose our own actions. The way we think and the choices we make can be made on the spot or through the experience of learning to fall, crawl, walk, or run. Either way, in the end, it is up to each individual to decide their own path.

GOOD VS. BAD

Despite the movies, there is no real battle between good and bad; each has its place. It's just a matter of balance and what we do with the good or bad thing in front of us. We all break down the things we learn, whether good or bad, and then process them. Here's how we basically process a good example:

> We observe the example, figure out the mechanism, try to copy it, verify results, and become proficient if the example works for us. Let's say a parent saves all their left-over change and puts it in the bank. Their child sees the discipline of saving this spare

change. If the parent goes further and shows the child how the savings grow, the child learns small sums deposited over time, accompanied by the power of compound interest, can result in a bank account with lots of digits. They may copy the parent by taking up the habit of saving change and depositing it in their account, just like their parent did. *Voilà!* A good example.

The learning process from a bad example is only slightly different. We add one additional step, (italicized letters) to the above process:

We observe, figure out the mechanism, *find the opposite*, try to copy the opposite, verify results, and become proficient if it works. For example, if a parent smokes like a chimney, their child may realize it's a life-threatening and expensive habit, and thus decided *not to smoke*. *Voilà!* A bad example turned into a good choice.

It only takes a simple decision by the learner to make a good or bad choice. A few years ago, my childhood best friend and I were reminiscing about growing up in Spokane and becoming best friends. Then he asked a serious question—one that truly enlightened me because I had never given it much thought until then.

Friend: "Why do you think you ended up the way you did?"

Me: (without hesitation) "Because of my mom and Reed Sensei."

Friend: "What about your dad?"

Me: "Other than teaching me to juggle, how to drive, never to look in a woman's purse, to always walk a lady on the inside of the curb, and introducing me to my martial arts instructor, my dad really had nothing to do with raising me after my parents' divorce."

Friend: "I totally disagree. I'd say you learned way more from your dad than you think."

Me: "No, seriously, other than a few basic skills, he was absent and doesn't deserve any credit."

Friend: "Blue, your dad taught you how not to treat people, how not to make poor choices, how not to behave, and how not to raise a child the way he did."

My friend was absolutely right. My dad had helped to lead me in a good direction by being a poor example. I truly wish he'd been a more integral part of my life, more of a positive guide to shaping my life as a man and as a father, but in the end, life had different plans for us.

Even though I chose not to follow my dad's path, what my friend said is true. I also believe many of us realize what we are good at and what we are not. I'd like to believe my dad knew he wasn't the greatest role model, so he decided the next best thing he could do was introduce me to someone he trusted who could fill those important shoes. By acknowledging his weakness and finding someone else to fill the father-figure role for me, he made the greatest sacrifice possible.

Subconsciously, knowing what to avoid and how not to act is just as important as knowing what to do and how to act properly. My friend helped me see that bad examples can be as valuable as good ones. This was a revelation to me. And I acquired a new superhero skill—learning from watching others. Actually, my real superhero skill is being able to learn from bad examples.

Leading by example, mentoring thousands of people, and becoming successful is hard and takes effort. Learning to learn from what others have done well has helped me along this path. And learning from their mistakes, negative attitudes, lack of planning, shady values, and misbehavior helps me limit the number of poor decisions I make.

MENTOR/MENTEE

This relationship may be out of this world, but Luke Skywalker used his father's ways as an example of what not to do. Luke learned from a bad example not to join the power of the Dark Side. Luke respected his father as a Jedi Knight, but he was unaware Darth Vader was his father. He only knew Vader as the man who betrayed and killed his father. By the end of the trilogy, Luke accepted Vader as his real father, and as a result, his hatred disappeared and transformed into hope and love. He believed there was still good in Vader and that he could redeem himself by returning to the Light. Luke knew he wanted nothing to do with the path his father took, so he chose to learn from his father's mistakes and become a more powerful Jedi than his father.

SUMMARY

We're all a product of, and learn from, both good and bad examples. Therefore, it is imperative to maintain a positive outlook on life no matter where we grew up, who our family is, where we went to school, or the job we have. In the end, we're all in control of the choices we make. We're friends, family, coworkers, parents, teachers, coaches, managers, and leaders. As such, we know that setting a good example is an important part of these relationships. But it's not always easy.

We would all prefer to be surrounded by perfection, but that is outside of reality. Good and bad examples surround us every day. What we learn from those examples and what we do with that information is what is important.

Follow the good and learn from the bad. It's helpful to use bad examples and behaviors to discover dangers to our personal growth and develop a smooth road to success. Looking at behaviors you find less than admirable may help you become aware of and focus on how you'd rather be, act, lead, and even be remembered. Become a better person and achieve greater success by having both negative and positive influencers to learn from.

The way you behave can leave a lasting impression, positive or negative, on everyone you meet. Setting a good example by being your authentic self is no guarantee those you reach will mimic you or become your clone. In the end, the way the pendulum swings may not always be in the same direction as you or someone else may like or want. They, like you, can see good and bad examples and decide whether to emulate them. But you do have the ability to control where your personal pendulum swings and where it stops.

ACTION STEPS

THINK

Truly think about why you are the way you are, how you ended up the way you did, why you make the choices you do, and what direction or path you've chosen because of life's influences. Write down your thoughts and conclusions below.

_____

_____

_____

_____

_____

Think about yourself and those you interact with daily. How can you hold one another accountable for leading in the right direction or by the right example?

_____

_____

_____

List three people in the columns below whom you have vowed to never act like. Now list five things you've learned from each of them (positive or negative).

Person 1	Person 2	Person 3
_____	_____	_____
1. _____	1. _____	1. _____
2. _____	2. _____	2. _____
3. _____	3. _____	3. _____
4. _____	4. _____	4. _____
5. _____	5. _____	5. _____

DO

Begin holding yourself and others accountable for leading as positive examples. How we think and make choices are two of our greatest powers. It is your choice to use them positively or negatively.

Surround yourself with, follow, and learn from those you love, admire, and respect. But be observant and willing to learn from any circumstances or examples as well. Become a better person, mentor, and leader by using both good and bad examples.

THE SUM OF 4

MENTOR • **DEVELOP** • EXECUTE • SUCCEED

CHAPTER 8
MAINTAINING FOCUS

"When walking, walk. When eating, eat."

— Zen Proverb

In the last chapter, I emphasized that sometimes the best lessons and inspiration come from the worst examples. Learning from a bad example is truly as valuable as learning from a good one. I think we can agree that it's important to be a good role model and surround ourselves with positive influences, but because we are all a mix of bad and good examples, we have to be aware that something can always be learned from everyone, even if we don't see those people as ideals.

This chapter's focus will be to show the benefits and importance of paying attention, being present in the now, and concentrating fully. I'll show that doing one activity with full attention is safer, more efficient, and strategic, than trying to haphazardly do several activities simultaneously.

Have you ever read the same chapter over and over and still felt like you had not read it? Being distracted by someone or something can certainly cause a multitude of missed or overlooked things that are important. Walking aimlessly through life or at work, or not seeing the purpose or benefits something can bring, certainly will not win many high achievement accolades either. Is it possible the root cause to feeling this lack of purpose or sense of not getting much out of something is because you aren't putting much into it?

We all can relate to situations in which we are unable to pay attention. Whether it is that you're bored, too tired, enjoy daydreaming, or are preoccupied by other things, it can be nearly impossible to keep your mind from wandering. Even when you know it is important to focus on or retain something, the ability to pay attention can be overwhelmingly difficult.

Losing focus prevents us from paying attention, which, in turn, makes it difficult and sometimes impossible to focus on the task at hand. We often lose focus without realizing we are even doing it—until it is too late. Maintaining a high level of concentration is very difficult when you're exhausted or bored. This lack of concentration or focus can be a big problem if it is not reestablished. Jack Canfield, co-author of the Chicken Soup for the Soul series, said it best, "Successful people maintain a positive focus in life no matter what is going on around them. They stay focused on their past successes rather than their past failures, and on the next action steps they need to take to get them closer to the fulfillment of their goals rather than all the other distractions that life presents to them."

The ability to stay focused is key to a successful life. Being easily distracted or losing focus can leave you unprepared to hear or learn some of the most important aspects of successfully surviving in this world. By becoming complacent and just going through the motions, and not properly focusing or paying attention, you risk major negative consequences.

THE SAFETY ANNOUNCEMENT

Many of us like to believe we can multitask like a supercomputer. But the evidence says otherwise. I, for one, would love to claim the ability to watch television while surfing the internet, safely talk or text while driving, or read a newspaper and eat waffles while discussing the *dark side of the Force*, all at once. It seems we can juggle several things at once, but dividing our attention in this way truly impairs performance and retention.

Let's look at an example of extreme complacency that most of us have witnessed. Although plane crashes or other types of aircraft emergencies are rare, I always pay attention to the flight attendant showing the proper way to react in an emergency, and I review the flight safety information card located in front of me. This attention to detail isn't out of love for reading laminated pamphlets or a deep desire to watch live performances, but rather, it's based on the guidance and advice of my wife, Heidi, who is a flight attendant and instructor herself.

I specifically focus on the part about how to correctly exit the plane and where those exits are located. This information takes only a few seconds to learn, including which direction to turn the handle that opens the door and what to do next. Exiting a plane sounds simple enough, but under pressure, this task could be overwhelming to anyone not prepared. Have you ever noticed the number of people who talk, play on their phones, read, and otherwise ignore the flight attendant during these safety briefings?

Fliers have become so complacent about their own and others' safety that the belief, "It will never happen to me," has become firmly embedded in their heads. They don't really understand the dangers of behaving routinely during an emergency. The safety announcement is pointless if no one is paying attention. Paying attention and staying focused, on and off the airplane, is imperative to staying safe and being prepared for life.

WAX ON, WAX OFF

When we think about learning, we tend to think the one being taught is doing the learning. However, the teacher and anyone else present can learn from what is being taught. Therefore, you're at a disadvantage if you zone out, selectively listen, or lose focus on what's being taught. If you focus intently and pay attention, you will learn to see opportunities you never saw before.

Like the safety announcement example, selective attention can and will have consequences, as author Lesley Kagen once wrote, "[T]hings can happen when you least expect them, so you always gotta be prepared. And pay attention to the details. The devil is in the details."

This quote brings me back to the fatigue of doing 400 reverse punches and letting my attention span become limited in class one evening. After I had finished my punches, it was time for my noodle-arms to hold the pad for my partner. I mistakenly used this time to take a mental and physical break.

Seeing that I wasn't paying attention, Reed Sensei abruptly stopped class. Knowing I was the root cause, the entire class looked at me with laser beam eyes—the kind that guide missiles to their destination. I'd unintentionally just become the center of attention, and I knew it wasn't the good kind of attention.

To my surprise, Reed Sensei asked, "What is your partner learning right now?"

I told him he was practicing proper technique, speed, power, and efficiency.

Reed Sensei nodded in agreement.

Phew. Relief showered down upon me. Praying to the martial arts gods and crossing my fingers saved me and the class from an obscene number of push-ups.

Just when I thought I was safe, he hit me—not literally—with another question: "And what are you learning?"

Caught off guard, yet still feeling a bit confident from my first answer, my sixteen-year-old self pressed my luck with a slightly cockier answer: "How to count."

Unfortunately, luck had now left my side. Immediate push-ups resulted for myself and the rest of the class.

After completing 100 agonizing and noodle armed push-ups, we attentively stood back up. What Reed Sensei said next stupefied me.

"Blue, you're not here to just hold the pad or serve as a rag doll for someone's punch. Even though you're just holding the pad and not doing the actual exercise (of punching), you are in fact learning! Just as much, if not more, than your partner. Every time you hold the pad or serve as the target is the time to pay the closest attention."

Reed Sensei had basically just pulled a scene straight out of *The*

Karate Kid where Mr. Miyagi explains to Daniel *San* his "Wax On, Wax Off" and "Paint the Fence" lesson. The entire time that Daniel *San* thought he was doing menial or mundane work for his teacher, he was actually learning the basics of effectively defending himself and responding to an attacker.

In a nutshell, both my partner and I were practicing different sides of the same movement. By punching, my partner was learning how to execute a reverse punch and improve his endurance. Meanwhile, I was learning how to take a punch, relax, respond correctly to an attack, center myself, balance, breathe efficiently, and read the signs of my opponent's intentions or how he telegraphed his movements in an attack.

However, because I wasn't paying attention, I was missing the point of the exercise and not learning the most practical and important lesson being taught. Like my dad at breakfast, I had been missing the Millennium Falcon myself. I needed to ask myself why I was in class. It certainly wasn't to be a punching dummy. I was there to learn and improve myself, period.

Becoming aware that I had missed important details made me realize I wasn't taking full advantage of life or my training. If I didn't pay more attention to what I was doing, not only would I continue doing push-ups, but, more importantly, I might miss or overlook something crucial that one day could be beneficial or even lifesaving. I was there for a reason, and it was my sole responsibility to pay attention, listen, observe, and get the most out of each lesson or situation that presented itself, even when I was not the puncher.

READ THE DIRECTIONS FIRST

Since then, I've tried to apply Reed Sensei's lesson on the importance of focus because, when someone is talking and it sounds like blah blah blah, I've realized it's not always just blah blah blah. Sometimes a gem is hiding in there, and if you don't pay attention, you'll miss it; then you might be upset or disappointed with the result.

A perfect example of the need to pay attention occurred when I was taking a final exam in college. The professor handed out the exams while the class sat quietly in the small, hard-as-rock, personal desks no normal human adult could sit in comfortably for longer than three minutes. He then told us to read the instructions first and then begin.

The directions must have been eight or nine sentences long and took up a quarter of the first page. As I glanced at the first page, I noticed the first question wasn't even asked until nearly halfway through the page. Almost everyone in class quickly scanned or skipped the directions, in hopes of finishing fast and being done with school for the year—everyone, that is, except me and a couple of other students.

I read the directions, not because I enjoy reading directions or because I'm a stickler for following the rules, but because of the way the teacher told us how to take the test. Something just stood out in his tone the way he said it. That, and the fact that the length of the directions felt a bit odd, made me think I should read them. I made it about three sentences into the paragraph before being completely shocked. College was more than a few moons ago for me, so please don't quote me on this, but the sentence basically read, "If you are reading this, please turn to the last page of the test and read the first few sentences on the top of the page."

Well, this was odd, but I did what it said, turning to the last page and reading from the top. It said:

> If you are reading this, please sit here quietly until the classroom's clock's minute hand is on the five. At that time, collect your things and hand in your exam. Without any conversation, exit the class and pat yourself on the back for following directions. Please enjoy your summer knowing you just aced the final exam.

Wait! Was this for real? I looked up to see if anyone else was having the same reaction as me. The clock read four minutes past the hour, so if this was legit, there was less than a minute to wait before handing in my test. For the briefest moment, I thought I was in an episode of *The Twilight Zone* or on hidden camera for a practical joke show.

When the minute hand hit the five, still thinking it could be a prank, I looked around at the other students whose heads were down, focused on their tests, adamantly answering the litany of questions. I didn't want to bring attention to the "Get out of jail free card" I'd just found. I tried to make eye contact with the instructor, but his eyes were focused on his desk. Without visual confirmation, I decided to take a chance, or quite possibly, the bait.

I slowly picked up my backpack, stood up from my desk, and walked with the speed of a sloth toward the professor's desk. Only two other students, looking as dumbfounded as me, made the peculiarly long trip to the professor's desk with me. We laid our tests down and quietly walked out of the classroom.

I'm not sure if any of the other students even noticed us leaving, but once the three of us were well outside the classroom, we all concurred that we had, in fact, read the same directions. As it turns out, the three of us had followed directions correctly, and we all aced our final. Good thing, too, because business calculus was not my strongest subject. Attention to detail certainly bumped up my grade, but it also made for a funny story.

Have you ever missed something or dropped the ball by not paying attention, being distracted, or losing focus on what is being explained or taught? One truth in this world is that what we decide to give our attention to ultimately becomes our priority.

We all face a fast-paced world with more distractions than our parents or their parents ever had. We can't hope to rely only on habit to improve our focus and attention. Instead, it takes a conscious effort, choice, and intent to harness our ability to focus. Whether we're holding a punching pad or an iPad, we have the choice and power to stay focused and soak up everything important.

MENTOR/MENTEE

The '80s film *The Karate Kid*, tells the story of a high school boy, Daniel LaRusso, who experiences problems adjusting to a new school and new life after moving to California. Truly afraid for his safety, because he is bullied and harassed by a gang of fellow students, he unwittingly befriends and is successfully mentored by karate master Mr. Miyagi. Miyagi doesn't resolve or solve LaRusso's problems for him. Instead, he accentuates LaRusso's strengths through unconventional teaching methods. Miyagi repeatedly explains that to protect himself, LaRusso must focus on what's at hand.

SUMMARY

Our attention is essentially binary; we can only focus well on one thing at any moment. Think back to my breakfast with Darth Vader. We can multitask to some degree, but we often delude ourselves about how good we really are at it. Therefore, concentrate on one thing at a time.

In today's highly connected world, you must define boundaries around what is worth your attention and what can blur your focus. Just because your smartphone notifies you of a new message doesn't mean you have to shift your focus to it. We should know better than to let distractions derail us from focusing all our attention on what truly matters to us.

In the punching example, I let my mind wander because I thought nothing could be learned from the activity. The stark reality was that the mere act of holding the pad was intended to condition my mind to become fully attentive and see all situations as learning opportunities.

Our attention creates our experience. Our decision of where to direct it has the power to make us happy or miserable, keep us safe, keep us from making costly mistakes, help us learn invaluable lessons, and become a high achiever. In a world where so many forces compete for our attention, it's more important than ever to develop the ability to overcome distractions! By focusing our attention, being resistant to worthless distractions, and not walking aimlessly through life, we avoid wasted time, thus becoming more productive and efficient.

ACTION STEPS

THINK

Besides the question you are reading at this very moment, what are you giving most of your attention to currently?

_____

_____

_____

_____

_____

List three repetitive distractions that hinder your momentum and how you can eliminate them.

1. _____
2. _____
3. _____

List two vital things or situations you missed, forgot, or didn't hear fully because your mind was somewhere else. They should be two things you would go back in time to tell your past self to focus and pay attention to.

1. _____
2. _____

Ask yourself, "If I am bored or tired of what I'm doing, why am I doing it?" How can you change this perspective to find value, benefit, and purpose in what you are doing?

_____

_____

_____

_____

DO

Every situation, moment, person you meet, class you take, or job you work has an endless supply of valuable information available to help you achieve greater success. You must pay attention and be open to understanding when these opportunities or lessons present themselves. When they do, you'll be prepared and ready to soak them up and use them for your own success.

Focus on what's at hand in the now. Make the effort to truly listen and pay attention to every moment and situation to extract the value of everything. Pick all the fruit available to choose from in front of you, and then move on to the next tree or climb higher.

Declutter your mind to be more productive. Leave your problems and irrelevant things at the door and focus on one activity at a time. Control this time and what you let distract you.

THE SUM OF 4

MENTOR · **DEVELOP** · EXECUTE · SUCCEED

CHAPTER 9
BEING PREPARED

"Before anything else, preparation is the key to success."

— Alexander Graham Bell

It's important to remember that you might miss what's most important if you don't maintain focus and pay full attention. Open your eyes and ears! Whether it's doing something you enjoy and value or just doing something asked of you that you don't really enjoy. Be open to learning and getting the most out of it because there's a lesson in almost everything you do. How you process those moments, and whether you let yourself become distracted or bored, will determine the height you choose to climb to as an individual.

The point of this chapter is that preparation is an essential, yet often neglected, part of succeeding in life and business. Practicing the art of preparation enhances self-discipline, strategic thinking, confidence, and mental flexibility. Being prepared is a state of mind and body readiness to perform whatever duty or action necessary. The act of becoming prepared requires us to discipline ourselves to make the time, effort, and sacrifice needed. Those who are truly prepared understand that failing is part of life. Therefore, they take it upon themselves to continuously build social and emotional skills, values, and qualities that will last a lifetime and prepare them to act.

Take a moment to consider how you go about preparing for your daily life. Do you overly prepare for your goals, dreams, and plans, or do you just attempt to wing it when the time comes? Perhaps you've experienced being caught off-guard, like having your hard drive inexplicably crash, even when you think you're properly prepared. How long or well do you prepare for a job interview, public presentation, or certification exam? Knowing what to expect, what customers want, or what problems may arise is a much more comfortable and relaxing feeling than not knowing. Especially when it comes time to need to know!

DEFINING PREPARATION

I would define preparation as being ready for whatever comes your way. It's being at least one or two steps ahead. It's an insurance policy for everything you do. Preparation is being able to deal with expected and unexpected situations. Preparation is, as Clint Eastwood said, using the unofficial slogan of the US Marines in the military film *Heartbreak Ridge*, the ability to, "Improvise, adapt, overcome."

Whether you have a basic supply of food and water in the event of a catastrophic event, practice for an upcoming speech in front of a mirror multiple times, or simply add weight to your bat while taking swings, preparation is the key to success. It gives you an advantage and a leg up. And as auto-racing legend Bobby Unser once said, "Success is where preparation and opportunity meet."

Opportunity will come in all forms, ways, and times throughout our lives, but the only way to seize it is by being properly prepared. If you're not ready, you will squander opportunities.

BEING PREPARED   139

As a personal trainer, I have an obligation to be prepared to answer my clients' questions and help them find the quickest, easiest, and safest path to their goals. The same holds true for keynote speaking, where it's my job to be fully prepared mentally and physically to address my audience with relatable, valuable, and memorable information.

Broadly speaking, there are two kinds of things to prepare for: the expected and the unexpected. Being prepared for either makes everything that happens something you've seen or have already played out in your mind.

Of course, it's easier to prepare for the things we can reasonably expect. If I have a photo shoot or acting job, I can prepare myself by arriving early, being fashionably dressed, well groomed, and familiar with my lines. If I'm delivering a speech to an organization or at a conference, I can be healthy and well rested, prepare or test my visuals, review the subject matter, and familiarize myself with the location and my audience.

The unexpected is much more difficult to prepare for because it's unknown. The unknown can be a question you can't answer, a tire blowing out at sixty miles per hour, technology breakdowns, or being told you have an incurable illness. Even for these unexpected things, though, one can still prepare.

When you don't know the answer, you can prepare by reading about all things related to that topic. You can stay connected by looking to your support system for outside knowledge or new ideas of where to look next. You continue to learn and expose your mind to different thoughts to help reduce the time and effort needed to deal with the unexpected. To succeed in expected and unexpected situations, prepare your brain and know you've done all the homework necessary to be as well prepared as you can be.

PREPARING THEM TO FAIL

A common criticism of today's younger generations—whether it's true or not—is that they are growing up ill prepared while thinking everything they do is worthy of praise or they are always winners. Passing out awards or handing out trophies to everyone who participates, makes people feel like winners.

This practice is counterproductive because it sets kids up to fail later in life, creating a helpless falsehood or facade of entitlement that can have lasting repercussions. And while I do remember my mother and Reed Sensei being endlessly supportive of my creative ideas and efforts when I was little, they both made a conscious shift as I got older and prepared to strike out on my own. Neither of them asked for my approval to transition from simple biased praise to true "adulting," but it happened regardless. Looking back, I'm grateful my mom and Reed Sensei thought alike about how to truly earn praise. Our daughter is young enough to be in the "effort equals praise stage," but my wife and I will surely follow Reed Sensei's lead as the stakes need to be raised for her as she grows older.

We all see our successes in our own kids, students, mentees, or employees because in some ways their successes reflect on us, as do their failures. But no matter how uncomfortable it is not to see them succeed, even though we have a vested interest in their performance, we need to be okay with them failing. If we aren't, we are rolling the dice with their future by increasing their odds at failing, becoming helpless, feeling incredibly entitled, and not knowing how to be self-reliant.

For parents, there's a real danger in becoming overly or excessively involved in our kids' day-to-day lives to protect them or help them succeed. College admission scandals are prime examples of over-parenting, or "helicopter parenting" that had the opposite of the desired effect. By becoming involved and shielding our children, the problem only compounds. It can potentially create a culture unable to problem solve, overcome challenges, or even be self-sufficient. As Moses Maimonides once said, "Give a man a fish and feed him for a day; teach a man to fish, and you feed him for a lifetime."

Let me be real and honest. Whether you're an employee, student, manager, parent, mentor, leader, or politician, the world we live in is tough and there are no free lunches. Teaching people that there are free lunches creates and enables a society filled with people who expect things they don't deserve, which sets them up to fail today, tomorrow, or in their future. That is unless you prepare yourself!

REAP WHAT YOU SOW

Reed Sensei would often say, "If you practice poorly, you will perform poorly when the time comes to put that practice into real action. By not practicing, studying, or training with full intent and purpose, in a game that really matters such as in a fight, the results will most likely result in the same outcome. Poor performance!" This was a kind way of saying I would lose if I didn't try to practice as if I were in a real-life situation.

Your successes depend on how you live your life. If you want to be a champion, you better train like one. Much like the old proverb says, "You reap what you sow." Whatever you put your time, talent, and energy into is what you get back. Living with full intention and purpose behind the things you do will reap priceless benefits, and you will see the long-term effects of your actions.

When Reed Sensei felt we, his students, were becoming complacent or losing interest, he would remind us to appreciate how lucky we were to be there. We were wasting the opportunity to learn from his lessons and sessions that were tailored to prepare us for the world's harsh realities. He consistently explained:

> It's your choice to be here. If you practice without purpose, be ready for a big wake up call. *Ding. Ding. Ding.* (He imitated the boxing ring bell.) If you're in trouble, I won't be there to save or protect you. I cannot and will not fight your fights for you! I'm not here to kiss or pamper your butts or let you believe you're better than you really are. You need to earn that. My job is to prepare you for the hard truths of life. No one owes you anything, and it is you who hold all the cards to your life.

When it comes down to it, the real world does not pull any punches and you need to be prepared with the proper experience to support yourself. You must apply yourself aggressively to implement what you learn!

IMMERSION IN SELF-DEFENSE

The best way to learn a language is to live in the country where it is spoken and immerse yourself in it. Immersion has been proven to be the most effective and fastest way to learn a new language because it completely involves and forces the learner outside their comfort zone to communicate solely in that language.

To demonstrate immersion in self-defense training, Reed Sensei would put us under extreme circumstances and simulations to create as close to an authentic fight as possible. This training helped guarantee an experience that would prepare us to react appropriately, if forced to, as if it were second nature. If we failed, it would bring to light cracks in our foundation and the need to practice and work harder to give our absolute best. While in a safe and controlled environment, we also gained the confidence to keep pushing through pain, anxiety, and fear, and learned the importance of never quitting or giving up.

The idea was that the way we learned and practiced while training would be the way we would respond in a real-life fight. The sad reality is most people don't live their life (train) with real focus, purpose, or intent. In a real fight or any uncomfortable situation, I don't know many attackers who will miss their target on purpose or simply fall and intentionally lose.

Reed Sensei was not just teaching us to punch, kick, and defend ourselves from our partner or an opponent. He was teaching his students to roll with the punches of life's challenges. Making sure we trained in the most realistic environment ensured this and gave us the necessary confidence. He was bringing his students to the edge of their comfort zones and capabilities to extract their maximum performances.

Japanese-born American cartoonist and comic book series creator Stan Sakai highlighted the importance of being prepared for anything because anything can happen, when he said, "A samurai should always be prepared for death—whether his own or someone else's." This quote is an extreme example, but it highlights the reality that we are not able to pick and choose what bad things happen in our lives.

Being mentally and physically prepared to fight our own fights, literally and figuratively, ensured we would stand firm in the face of difficult challenges, have the will to endure, and never quit. Letting us win, giving us a free pass, or the ability to slip by was counterintuitive to Reed Sensei's values and his belief that one must be fully prepared for all things that happen outside the dojo! I still have a slightly crooked nose from a foot or fist connecting to it over the years during the simulation training.

Reed Sensei was teaching us to spread our wings and learn to fly like a bird on our own. Each time, we increased the distance we could fly, through new skills attained, experiences we experienced, and with better physical and mental endurance. Every day, we would fly just a little farther, higher, or longer, proving to ourselves and others that we could do it with earned confidence and on our own.

We can't be afraid to let our children, youth, or even employees take flight on their own. We're supposed to let them become independent, gain confidence, and make names for themselves. I think the biggest gift we can give them is the ability to spread their wings and fly on their own. By doing this, they can discover who they are and explore confidently what the world has to offer, how they can contribute to it, and most importantly, how to be properly prepared for it.

MENTOR/MENTEE

Actor and director, Clint Eastwood was mentored by his grandmother, who encouraged him to always work hard and pursue his dreams. She helped him realize his potential and inspired him to put the effort and time in to be truly prepared for life and any venture Eastwood wanted to take on. He once said, "I've had many mentors in my life…my grandmother…was always encouraging. She always thought I was going to be something, when nobody else, including myself, thought I was going to amount to anything."

SUMMARY

Ultimately, you have a duty to come prepared for anything that matters to you. Lack of preparation is the surest way to fail. There are no excuses, and no free lunches, but neither are there any obstacles that can truly keep you from fulfilling your dreams. There is always a way around, over, underneath, or through the obstacle, if you are prepared. Putting in the hard work and preparation required for expected and unexpected events is the ultimate path to becoming confident and fluent in the art of preparation.

Practicing what I preach and walking the walk in the eyes of thousands of clients or students, while acting or modeling, and with my stage presentations, all matter to me. I'm always learning, and I am far from perfect, but by preparing again and again for each new situation, I get better, become more confident, can deliver better results, and am better prepared for the future.

Yes, success takes sacrifice, time, and money and can lead to long, tiresome hours, but if you aren't willing to do the hard work of preparing, then you shouldn't take on the task in the first place. If, however, you have taken on something, you must own that obligation, be willing to immerse yourself in it, and prepare for it so you can really deliver when it truly counts.

When you put your knowledge to the test by taking action, you get true confirmation of the actual level of understanding you possess. No one will fight your battles with more passion, vigor, or devotion than you!

ACTION STEPS

THINK

Would you consider yourself an avid preparer, the worst procrastinator, or somewhere in between? Write down two things you could do better to prepare more or procrastinate less.

_____

_____

List two times in the past when you could attribute your success directly to being well-prepared.

_____

_____

List a time when being ill-prepared resulted in a much less desirable outcome. If you could go back in time to properly prepare yourself, what would you do differently?

_____

_____

What knowledge, skills, relationships, or experiences are missing or need development for you to be better prepared to succeed with your goals?

_____

_____

List three things you feel are important for you to achieve success in the next year, three, and five years.

1. _____
2. _____
3. _____

Now take those three things and write three steps required for achieving each one.

1. _____
2. _____
3. _____

DO

Immerse yourself by preparing 100 percent in the things you value most and want to succeed at. Make a commitment to yourself to always train for the real world because, sometimes, there's no second chance.

Keep rising and falling, while picking up important lessons along the way to improve. Some experience will come from your mistakes, some from watching and learning from others, and some through research and from simply reading.

Walk the walk and talk the talk. Practice what you preach. Remember, if you practice badly, you will perform badly. A significant difference exists between practical and theoretical experience. Put what you learn into practical situations and proactively prepare each day for both the expected and unexpected.

THE SUM OF 4

MENTOR • **DEVELOP** • EXECUTE • SUCCEED

CHAPTER 10
BEING AFRAID

"You gain strength, courage, and confidence by every experience in which you really stop to look fear in the face. You are able to say to yourself, 'I have lived through this horror. I can take the next thing that comes along.' You must do the thing you think you cannot do."

— Eleanor Roosevelt

Ultimately, as we discussed in Chapter 9, the mentor/mentee relationship prepares you to take flight on your own because you are prepared to face expected and unexpected obstacles. In the end, you have the power to choose your life's direction because you are the pilot, flying your plane.

Now, we will peer into how my key mentor successfully guided me through my fears. Because fear is part of being human, the goal of this next chapter will be to develop a plan to face, accept, overcome, and learn what fear and failure can teach us. We will also learn how to transform and harness the angst and tension that accompanies fear to our advantage.

Fear of change, the unknown, failure, public speaking, being physically hurt, loneliness, or not having enough time can feel like a Category 5 hurricane to many. Maybe your fear is a lack of confidence in your ability to sell something, speak publicly, manage, parent, or lead others. It could be a fear of someone, something, or a combination of both. Or maybe it's something from your past that could come back to haunt you. What triggers your fear?

FEAR IS...

Fear comes in many forms. It is an emotional response induced by a perceived threat, which can cause a change in the brain and behavior. Everyone confronts many types of fear throughout life. Those fears may arise from a confrontation, from avoiding a threat, or in the form of a new discovery. No matter what fear you encounter, if you're like me, fear can lead you to hide, run away, or become as frozen as Han Solo in carbonite.

Fear is said to be the most powerful emotion known to humankind—even more powerful than love. That's because our very survival depends on it. It's triggered in the most primitive part of our brain, the part responsible for alerting us to and protecting us from danger. Fear keeps us safe by triggering the fight or flight response.

All that said, fear lives in your mind. Your fear is always about what's going to happen next. It is an unpleasant emotion caused by the belief that someone or something is dangerous and likely to cause pain. As scary as fear is, it's also a normal emotion that everyone has and feels.

Whether you can't stand heights, hate small spaces, won't travel by airplane, avoid opening the bills, pass out when you see blood, or hate snakes like Indiana Jones, fear is as much a part of all our lives as the air we all breathe. How we should breathe that fear in and what we do with it is best described by American novelist

Chuck Palahniuk when he wrote, "Find out what you're afraid of and go live there."

INTIMIDATION

Many of us have experienced the fear of getting hurt, getting in a physical fight, or being bullied or picked on. Feeling threatened or intimidated by someone we're afraid of who may emotionally or physically hurt us results from overplaying and comparing in our mind their accomplishments or physical stature to ours.

For nearly a decade, a sister karate school in proximity to ours would often visit and train with us at our dojo. The school was led by a young instructor who was, at that time, a fifth-degree black belt and an amazing practitioner of *Shotokan karate*. He was strong as an ox and the epitome of a mesomorph. Basically, he would have served as the perfect model for a Michelangelo statue. With his cat-like reflexes and extremely effective and efficient technique, he could have been an Olympic athlete.

Many martial art schools, depending on their instructor(s), are known for being more geared toward either self-defense, traditional practice, or *randori* (sparring). Well, his school was known for its love of physical sparring and for placing first in tournaments. Whether it was for school bragging rights or the students' egos, training with them always came with plenty of bruises.

In the '80s martial arts movie *The Last Dragon*, the main character's arch nemesis is named Sho'nuff. He has a teaching style and attitude much like the head instructor of Cobra Kai in *The Karate Kid*, as well as our sister school's sensei. If you haven't seen this cult classic, please put this book down momentarily to google what

I'm referencing. Next, please add *The Last Dragon* to your watch list so this travesty is quickly remedied. Great, now let's continue.

Our sister school's sensei was tough as nails and ranked as one of the best karate competitors in the US. If anyone could catch bullets in his teeth, it was this guy. Parts of his teaching style differed and contradicted Reed Sensei's because he directly or indirectly taught through intimidation and inflicting physical pain to impart certain lessons. He was incredibly superior to me and any other student at our dojo at karate. I was very intimidated and scared of his ability to hurt me because he could kick my butt blindfolded if he wanted to.

Once, when I was seventeen, I vividly remember sparring against him when he kicked me in the head, knocking me to the ground and nearly out cold. Then he said, "Ya gotta learn to duck."

Let's face it; if you're getting punched or kicked in full contact, it's painful, and you're going to be afraid. There's no way to get around that. Whatever might hurt you can and will scare you as well. Getting beat up doesn't make you a better fighter. Sure, it might make you tougher, but it also might make you a more psychologically damaged fighter. Personally, my ego could only take so much abuse before my self-esteem and confidence would become damaged.

I felt ill every time our school sparred against this school and instructor and would secretly cross my fingers before each class, hoping they wouldn't attend or visit that class. Year after year, my heart continued to sink to the floor every time because I anticipated the shame, humiliation, and pain of getting hurt. Besides the angst and fright, class with them was just peachy.

KAPOW! TWHACK! WHAM!

Even as a black belt in my late teens, sparring with the students from the sister school and their instructor was last on my list of things I looked forward to practicing in class. One evening, after the other school arrived, Reed Sensei started class with everyone sparring for timed rounds! Anxiety and knots began to build in my stomach as I sparred other students and my turn to spar their sensei drew closer and closer. Because Reed Sensei supervised the class, everyone would have a chance to spar each other, as well as with the other instructor. As one of the black belt students, he would turn up his A-game with me and the beating of *Blue Stiley* would commence sooner than later.

As my round with the instructor approached, I could see him out of the corner of my eye preparing to warm up for our round. I began sweating profusely, like I was under a heat lamp in the middle of a North Carolina summer. My heart beat faster than a speeding bullet.

Finally, it was our turn. *Ding, ding, ding*—the fictitious bell rang. After successfully blocking my every feeble attempt to proactively attack and score against him, he decided play time was over and stopped toying with me. Faster than I could react, he unleashed a side kick with the sound of a lightly wet whip. It connected like a punch straight out of a Batman comic to the right side of my ribs—*kapow!*

I felt like I'd just been thrown from a horse and landed on my back, knocking the wind right out of me. *I seriously just broke or cracked a rib*, I thought. The round finished, and we had a couple of minutes to rest before picking up where we left off. This really meant I had a few moments to collect my breath and check to see if all my ribs were still in place.

Nearly in tears from utter fear and what felt like his left foot still embedded in my ribcage, I thought, *Enough is enough*. I was tired of being scared and wanted to gain as much control of my own fear as I could. So, with a trembling voice, and possibly a broken rib, I gathered my courage and asked the source himself why I always lost to him.

Expecting him to say because he outranked me or that I was just not good enough, his actual answer shocked me. I will forever remember what he said in his thick Brooklyn accent:

> You really want to know, huh? Well, son, you are afraid of me. Blue, I've already won and beaten you before I even walk through these doors. Every time I come here, I intentionally look you in the eyes and note how you react. At that moment, I can read the fear in your eyes, and I know beating you physically will be easy because I've already taken you mentally. You're broken well before I ever spar with you. You've already given up! Your face and head drop in complete surrender. You might as well be waving a white flag in the air when I walk in.

Well, he had answered my question and taken constructive criticism to a whole new depth. Brutal honesty aside, he was absolutely right. I can say without a doubt that whenever I saw him through the front windows of the dojo, my confidence left me, and I let fear control my emotions. My head would drop out of pure disappointment, as if I were practicing my bowing skills. Only I wasn't bowing. He had already won without delivering a single punch or kick.

Reality was built on my own thoughts. What I thought, I became, and what I imagined, I was creating. The mental power he held over me took me back nearly ten years to the exact same emotions

I had felt toward my childhood bully. He was just a bigger, stronger, and a much more lethal opponent than the bully was. But I knew that, just like with the bully, I didn't want him to have that control over me. Of course, getting him out of my head and regaining that control was easier said than done.

MIND CONTROL

Trying not to think about something is not easy, especially when it's something you fear. To consider the futility of saying "Don't think about something," let us try an old, simple mind exercise:

Do not imagine a pink elephant.

What happened when you read the sentence above? Odds are, unless you never fall for the "old Jedi mind trick," you did the very thing I asked you not to do and thought of a pink elephant. How disappointing is that? You could have thought of Mickey Mouse, shapes in the clouds, or even your mom's baked cookies (in my case, her bacon waffles). You had infinite options, but you still disobeyed my simple request. Don't worry; I'm going to give you one more chance. Let's try this experiment one more time. Ready?

Do not imagine a pink elephant in a white karate uniform kicking Mickey Mouse's ears while on top of a giant cumulus cloud.

You did it again, didn't you?

What you just experienced was an example of how easy it is to persuade or lead the human mind. Consider a baseball player experiencing a hitting slump—not a single hit in the last twenty-three times at bat. Besides possibly being benched, the player would recite the same mantra, "Don't strike out, don't strike out, don't strike out," every time they were on deck. Then the batter faces the pitcher and inevitably strikes out because he's unable to reorient his thoughts to something desirable, like a home run.

So, what's the effect of all this rumination? Effectively, I'd thought about getting beat up every time I faced the other sensei and let doubt, intimidation, and fear stay at the top of my mind. The cards were already stacked against me, because in my mind, I'd already defeated myself well before ever stepping onto the mat. Hence, I would never win or even score against him. I was letting my mind take control of the "what ifs," of getting hurt. Guilty 1,000 percent.

After that evening, four things happened: 1) I never looked at fear the same way because I began to accept it, 2) I was cautious but never feared that instructor again, 3) I gained a newfound respect for him because of his positive criticism and encouragement to master my fear of him, and 4) I learned a fight can be won before it even begins, or better yet, without ever throwing a punch.

MENTOR/MENTEE

Virgin Group founder Richard Branson understands the importance of surrounding yourself with those you can benefit and learn from, and who can help guide you. Branson asked English airline entrepreneur Sir Freddie Laker for guidance in getting his struggling Virgin Atlantic over its struggles. Today, Branson credits his success to having a helping hand while getting started and knowing he never settled or gave up, due to Laker's successful mentoring. Branson once said, "If you ask any successful businessperson, they will always say they have had a great mentor at some point along the road."

SUMMARY

Fear is expressed in a wide variety of ways: fear of change, fear of getting older, fear of public speaking, fear of being caught, fear of failing as a startup company. Fear will always exist and surround us. We all have similar fears, but they're unique to each individual's relationship to fear. How we deal with fear is what differs.

Remember, the lens through which you see and navigate your life will affect all you think, see, believe, and do. You will be afraid. You will be intimidated. Everyone, even the most successful and highest achievers, experience these feelings because they are part of life. Being aware and accepting your fears, rather than hiding from them, is the first step to confronting them. Taking what you can from them and learning to control them, instead of being controlled, is the ultimate strategy to overcome what frightens you. Controlling them, in turn, results in knowing you're living without regret or compromise. You are in control!

ACTION STEPS

THINK

What are you most afraid of today, and does it differ from when you were a kid or young adult?

_____
_____
_____
_____

How do you face your fears? Do you run, hide, give up, avoid, or distract yourself, or do you walk up to it and say, "Enough is enough"?

_____

_____

List three things you've feared but no longer fear. Now, make a list of two things you did to overcome each of those fears. You should have six remedies at the end of this exercise unless they overlap.

1. Fear: _____

   Overcame by: _____

   Overcame by: _____

2. Fear: _____

   Overcame by: _____

   Overcame by: _____

3. Fear: _____

   Overcame by: _____

   Overcame by: _____

Identify the three things you're most afraid of right now. Apply your six remedies from your past fears to decide if they are out of your control or are something you can overcome and take control of. Take your time answering each fear.

1. Fear: _____

   How to overcome: _____

   How to overcome: _____

2. Fear: _____

   How to overcome: _____

   How to overcome: _____

3. Fear: _____

   How to overcome: _____

   How to overcome: _____

DO

If you can't control the fears you filled in above, then let go of them and move on to the fears you can control.

Change your perception of whatever you're afraid of and begin to accept it. Consistently ask yourself how you would act if there were no ramifications to acting against fears you encounter in the future. Reality is built on your own thoughts. What you think, you will become. What you imagine, you will create.

Fear being in the exact same place or position next year as you are today!

Don't let your mind or someone else control you and your emotions. Talk about your fears with someone you trust for advice. Be honest.

PART III
EXECUTE

4

MENTOR • DEVELOP • **EXECUTE** • SUCCEED

CHAPTER 11
FAILING 101

"Do not be embarrassed by your failures;
learn from them and start again."

— Richard Branson

To recap our journey so far, in Part I of this book, we looked at the importance of surrounding ourselves with influential mentors and leaders to help bring out our best. The strongest connection and main driving factor between a mentor and a mentee is the result of R.E.L.A.T.E. (respect, wish to emulate, love, admire, trust, and empathy from both parties). In Part II, we delved into ways to begin developing the core lessons, strategies, and formulas to push yourself to a higher level. The two-way relationships and connections are the cornerstones to achieving success. They help us gain the confidence required to develop the skills necessary to improve ourselves, strengthen our mind, learn from others' experiences and mistakes, take chances, and overcome our fears. Now, we will begin using fear to our advantage and putting these strategies into action to formulate and create your life-changing experience.

Fear is normal. Instead of letting fear control you, learning to harness its power and control it is the ultimate weapon. In the last chapter, we learned the importance of accepting what you're afraid of and how to move past those fears. Now, we'll look at one of the biggest fears—fear of failure—which underlies most fears and often prevents us from taking action, even when it's in our best interest. Fear of failure can be immobilizing. However, our only real limits are self-imposed. We all want to avoid failing, but no great success has ever come without at least one, and more often multiple, epic failures. Letting your fear of failure stop you from taking action to achieve your goals might be the greatest failure of all.

Do you ever put anything off or avoid something because you don't want to take a chance of failing or feeling embarrassed, or because the cost may be too high? If so, it's time to take a chance and act because most of your fears are baseless and, in your mind, rather than part of reality.

TAKE A CHANCE

Please honestly answer these two questions: 1) What's the harm in trying something new? 2) What's the worst thing that could happen if you took a chance? The short answer to both is: You could fail. Although failure can be painful, it's a normal part of life that can unlock great potential. But to do so, we must change our mindset about what failure means.

Rather than seeing failure as detrimental, we need to use it as a reminder to get back on track, learn from our mistakes, and try again. We must convert failure into a tool for success that teaches us what works and what doesn't. As Dale Carnegie, author of *How to Win Friends and Influence People*, wrote, "Take a chance! All life is a chance. The man who goes farthest is generally the one who is willing to do and dare."

Taking a chance or chances on opportunities, even when you're scared of failing, paints a much clearer picture of your wants, needs, and dreams in all things. Society might not reward defeat, but it sure does reward those who take a chance. Momentum forward always starts with a single step grounded to be better, do better, or get closer to a goal. Failure is part of life; it helps you grow, become stronger, and learn from your mistakes. Taking a chance at anything uncharted, with small steps toward your goal, will increase your confidence and help you overcome the fear of failing horribly. As hockey great Wayne Gretzky once said, "You miss 100 percent of the shots you don't take."

LEMONS INTO LEMONADE

In the mid-1980s, the sports card industry was booming. Card shops were popping up everywhere, and card shows took place regularly at major hotels and convention centers all across the US. Even *The Wall Street Journal* and *The New York Times* began pushing baseball cards as the next best investment, comparing them to stocks and bonds. And just like many major stock market bull runs, no one believed the market would drop because card values were going up faster than people could purchase them. Adults told horror stories of their parents throwing away their shoebox collections filled with rare and priceless cards, while others wished they hadn't used their cards in bicycle spokes to create a motor sound. Everyone, including many of my fellow middle school students, were jumping on the band wagon to create a priceless collection of their own, to trade, make money, invest, and collect the most mint condition cards possible. I was no different.

For some reason, I've always had an aversion to chocolate. I'm not allergic to it, nor would I explode from eating it, I just have never enjoyed its taste. In middle school, I turned that aversion to my advantage by selling my chocolate milk each day to other kids for twenty-five cents. After two days, I then took that fifty cents and bought a fifty-cent pack of baseball cards, at a convenience store on my way to school. I took something I didn't like and turned it into something I did. Lemons into lemonade!

That same day, as I was selling my carton of milk, someone offered me seventy-five cents for my unopened pack of cards. Since I knew I could just buy another pack on my way home that day, I accepted their offer. That sale, plus another chocolate milk sale, left me with $1.00 to purchase two more packs later that day. The next day of school commerce was no different, and my returns began to increase, thus allowing me to buy more and more packs each day. As you can imagine, my buying power increased, and my profits began to snowball in my favor. To save you from doing the math, by day twelve of chocolate milk sales and sport card packs, I was bringing in more than sixty dollars. The power of compounding.

I continued this locker and lunchroom racketeering business for nearly a month, selling a variety of sports cards, and eventually having to hit several stores to and from school to keep up with the demand from my classmates. That is, until the vice principal caught wind that I was selling something out of my locker. It wasn't drugs, but my little card business got chopped, forcing me to create a new strategy for my sports cards venture.

This new strategy took me out of my comfort zone—but being a kid with no debt, I had nothing to lose. So, I got my first business license and became an *uber*-young entrepreneur. With my mom as the chauffeur, I used my newly acquired business license to become a vendor and attend the local card shows, sublet my table space to my friends to sell their cards, and devised fun games to attract my peers. At age twelve, with no overhead or employees, I could undercut my competitors' prices and still make huge profits. Parents pulled out their wallets, but ultimately, I was a kid marketing and selling to other kids.

My little sports card business lasted until 1991, when I began high school and schoolwork became a priority. Thankfully, I got out when the card industry was at its peak and before the bottom fell out and card values of overproduced cards crashed. As a result of thinking outside the box, not being afraid to fail, and taking the chance to join the ranks of adult business owners, I successfully accumulated and saved enough to pay for my entire college education, room, board, and even books. I also kept the oldest, most expensive, and rarest cards that never lost their value for my own collection, which even after adjusting for inflation, I plan on using for my daughter's future college education.

COLLEGE IN JAPAN

Let's face it; when we're afraid to do something, it's easier for most of us to avoid doing it. We tend to focus on not failing or making a mistake so much that we don't aim for anything greater, thus settling for a life of mediocrity. I understand firsthand the aversion to putting in the extra work required or having to experience undo strain, pressure, and stress. The road less traveled can hurt more, take more effort, and be filled with nasty obstacles.

However, if we never take a chance, we can never be more than average. Fear of failure can't be allowed to control our momentum forward. Thomas Edison never saw his road to the invention of the lightbulb as a path of failures. Instead, he said, "I haven't failed. I've just found 10,000 ways that won't work."

It's all about how you perceive failure. From fear of the possibility of being wrong, Japanese students are infamous for not raising their hands to answer questions during class, even if they know the correct answer. In their culture, standing out in general is pictured as going against the grain. "Losing face" or the shame associated with failure is too great. So, to avoid causing students shame if their answer is incorrect, it is typical that Japanese teachers don't even call on students.

By contrast, American students consider being called upon a nuisance, but normal. Although, for them, not knowing the answer can be embarrassing, it just doesn't hold the same weight as it does in Japan. It also gives teachers an opportunity to correct the student and to know where their own teaching might need adjustment.

When I attended college in Tokyo, my courses were taught in Japanese, and I was often the only non-native speaker in class. My marketing class was taught by a Japanese teacher fluent in English. During one of his lectures, he was describing the importance of accuracy in branding and marketing Japanese products in Japan versus Western countries. Midway through the lecture, he said a word that sounded like "gooosu" or "guusuu."

I like to think I'm fluent in Japanese, but sometimes I have no idea what a word means. So, when I heard "guusuu," my head tilted to one side like a confused dog. My reaction caught the teacher's attention, and going against the norm of not involving the class, he turned to me and asked, "Stiley, s*an, gusu wakarimasuka*?" ("Do you know what "guusuu" means, Mr. Stiley?")

Since I didn't know, unlike my Japanese classmates, I figured there was no harm in guessing. The Japanese language, like many others, adopts certain words from other languages. For example, the words door, fork, and telephone were adopted from English, in large part, because these items didn't exist in Japan until they were introduced to them via Western cultures. In Japanese, the meanings of these words are the same, but the pronunciation is just a little different.

Knowing this, I figured there was a slight chance that "guusuu" was a word adopted from English. I thought it sounded like goose, and since I didn't know what the word goose was in Japanese, the chance of it being the same word seemed plausible.

I took the chance and replied, "*Ookii ahiru desuka*?" (Is it a big duck?) I knew the word for duck in Japanese. Perhaps this answer teetered on stupid, but I thought, *Why not*? I could be helping other students if they didn't know the meaning either, right?

Well, I was wrong. And the teacher—fluent in English as he was—nearly came to tears with laughter. Teachers laughing out loud is also a Japanese rarity, so I knew I was incorrect. However, when he explained to the class what was so funny and why I'd answered the way I had—the words sounded alike or similar—the entire class erupted in laughter—very not typical.

While everyone was laughing, I used my Japanese-English dictionary and looked up "*Gusu*." I hadn't even been close! It meant "even number." The laugh was certainly on me, and as a result, my classmates nicknamed me "*Ooki Ahiru*" or "The big duck." The name stuck for the rest of the year.

Okay, so I got made fun of, but on the bright side, I learned a new word and I have a great story to share that helps people see the importance of not being afraid to take a chance. I learned from it, improved my Japanese, and later used this story to successfully win a scholarship while living there. As Henry Ford famously said, "Failure is simply the opportunity to begin again, this time more intelligently."

Making myself the center of attention hasn't always been easy for me. However, because I learned that standing out and failing at something was not catastrophic, I was able to change what failure meant for me. It may be embarrassing, unfortunate, sometimes expensive, and even hurtful, but failure is certainly not detrimental. We can't let that first step toward doing something new or taking a chance be the most difficult task or thing to fear.

SMALL STEPS

Fear of failure can be so paralyzing it can prevent you from moving forward to achieve your true goal. Taking the first step is the most important effort you can take, and it can be accomplished more easily by being less afraid of potential outcomes. The hardest part is having the discipline and mindset to pick yourself up again and again after failing to get back on track—each time with more confidence and wisdom to achieve greater success. As Abraham Lincoln once said, "My great concern is not whether you have failed, but whether you are content with your failure."

Failing early, when the consequences are minimal, makes it easier to become less afraid of risk or making mistakes. For example, if I forgot my karate uniform, I would have to train in street clothes—doing 300 front kicks or side kicks in jeans is very uncomfortable to say the least, but manageable for a couple of hours. Another example—if I defied my parents by not eating what they put in front of me, I might go to bed hungry with a growling stomach. It might hurt for a bit, but I'd eventually doze off and be able to eat in the morning.

In either case, as a youngster, I learned from these small failures, and in turn, was smarter the next time and less afraid to mess up. I began to see it was okay to fail, make mistakes, take chances, and even fall.

You just can't give up if you do fail. Instead, learn from mistakes to become stronger. As Napoleon Hill, author of *Think and Grow Rich*, said, "Most great people have attained their greatest success just one step beyond their greatest failure."

Is avoiding risk worth knowing in your heart that you're settling and taking the easier path? Taking a chance means giving up some control, but that doesn't translate to being out of control. Learning from past failures and mistakes lets you move through your fear of failing. You must still weigh all possibilities, envision the best outcomes, and proceed with small, intelligent steps to make an educated decision. I assure you, not taking chances is the surest way to keep you from succeeding.

MENTOR/MENTEE

Baseball Hall of Fame legend Cal Ripken, Jr. looked to his father, Cal Ripken, Sr., as a powerful mentor. Ripken played under his father's management for the Baltimore Orioles and credits his father for his values and for helping him break through small failures and fears, like being sent back down to the minors or having long hitting slumps in the big leagues. Ripken, Jr. knew the value of a mentor. "The value of a mentor…I don't know what value you can place on it, but the right words spoken at the right time from a person that's been through it before…can make all the difference…."

SUMMARY

Fear of failure can be paralyzing, but you can't let it stop you from moving forward. People who suffer from fear often subconsciously undermine their own efforts to avoid disappointment or failure. We mustn't let fear stop us from taking the chance to improve ourselves. Everyone experiences growing pains and fails, plain and simple. Taking what we can learn from our mistakes and errors, not settling for mediocrity, and using new information and experience is the only way to achieve success beyond your current abilities. If you want different results, you must change the approach.

ACTION STEPS

THINK

Write down three things you have avoided doing or starting because you were afraid of taking a chance or afraid of what the outcome could be.

1. _____
2. _____
3. _____

Think of all the times you've crashed and burned. What knowledge or experience did you gain that took you a step closer to becoming a wiser person? Write five of those things down.

_____

_____

_____

_____

_____

DO

Use your fear to push yourself even harder. Take control of your fear of failing and change your mindset. The inner voice of reason, belief, and confidence must drown out fear. Take small steps when taking chances; be careful and intelligent about doing so.

Continuously make lists of things you don't want to do or are afraid to do. Challenge yourself and start tackling those tasks daily, monthly, and annually. Start chopping away at those things. Begin crossing them off your list.

Fail until you cease to fail. Then, after success, go take on a new challenge and be prepared to fail some more.

Don't be afraid to fail because it is part of the process, not the end. Everyone does it. Be more than just average! Recite this daily, "No one ever got ahead in life by settling for average."

4

MENTOR • DEVELOP • **EXECUTE** • SUCCEED

CHAPTER 12
EMBRACING CRITICISM

"We need very strong ears to hear ourselves judged frankly, and because there are few who can endure frank criticism without being stung by it, those who venture to criticize us perform a remarkable act of friendship, for to undertake to wound or offend a man for his own good is to have a healthy love for him."

— Michel de Montaigne

In the last chapter, we discussed what it means to fail. Although failure can be painful, it is part of life, and if used correctly, failure can be the most important key to achieving our greatest successes. The worst that can happen when you take a chance is that you fail. It can hurt, but it's usually not detrimental. On the flipside, by taking a chance, you could create the next lightbulb, iPhone, or cure for cancer!

In this chapter, we are going to break down what being criticized means, what it can do to us, and how to use that criticism to improve ourselves. Not all criticism is equal, and its validity depends on who it comes from and in what context. Accepting and embracing constructive criticism from a respected influence, such as a mentor, can serve as a sneak peek into your weaknesses and will be a crucial factor in giving you a competitive advantage.

Does hearing something bad about yourself sometimes make you want to roll your eyes, make you angry, or even make you clench your fists and become defensive? Being criticized can surely make your blood boil and cause you immediately to defend or counter it. Have you ever quit or wanted to quit because you were criticized? If the answer is yes, you can understand criticism can be harsh. But recognizing this doesn't fix or make things better. What makes them better is understanding the motive behind it and learning how to accept criticism gracefully.

CRITICISM CREATES OPPORTUNITIES

Accepting and hearing negative feedback, even if it's entirely accurate and constructive, can be difficult. The moment we hear a critique, negative or positive, our heartbeat quickens and our mind begins to race. You might ask, *Why does it feel this person is assaulting me?* Then you immediately look for a retort to rationalize whatever actions are being questioned.

Sometimes, we can be our own worst critics. Criticism is painful because it brings into question what we believe about ourselves and our own worth. When we are criticized, we feel it's a statement about who we are. It can lead to doubt, and worst of all, cause us to quit.

Negative criticism can sting something fierce. Even constructive criticism stings! It hurts because it's true, and as the late actor and comedian Leslie Nielsen said, "Truth hurts. Maybe not as much as jumping on a bicycle with a seat missing, but it hurts."

Many of us don't want to admit how important being criticized can be, but how else can we identify our weaknesses? We're not all

God's gift to everything or everyone else, and none of us are perfect. We're all fallible, with room to grow in our successes, relationships, parenting, mentoring, and leadership.

Growing in these ways, however, requires we accept a certain truth. That truth is: To make ourselves better and more successful, we must be open to criticism, accept that we are sometimes wrong, and be open to change.

KEEPING UP WITH THE BLACK BELTS

My teenage years were some of the most influential and memorable times I had with Reed Sensei. I was truly a sponge then. I loved to soak up everything this man had to teach, advise, and mentor me on. During that time, I also became very proud of my discipline and dedication, how I trained, and how martial arts was physically sculpting my body.

Training became my priority, and I cherished the opportunity to train with someone I aspired to be like and connected with R.E.L.A.T.E. I enjoyed it so much that I even started school an hour early so I could have an extended lunch period, thus giving me time for an extra karate class every day.

The combination of an early start and extended lunch allowed me to finish the school day with everyone else, partake in after school sports, and most importantly, have time for a second, longer judo or karate class in the evening. To say I packed my day would be true, but it was all self-inflicted and certainly didn't overwhelm me. In fact, balancing this "go, go, go" lifestyle, while still succeeding academically, became a fun challenge—a challenge I still enjoy practicing today. I never felt like it was too difficult or became a burden.

I would have trained 24/7 if allowed.

Partaking in the midday black belt class was a big deal. First and foremost, it was exclusively for black belts, and I wasn't a black belt. I was a year or so away from testing for my first-degree black belt, but I knew one of the best ways to improve was to train with a wide range of people, especially those better than you. This practice is similar to the language immersion example in Chapter 9. The problem was most of the advanced students only practiced during the midday class.

Therein lay the dilemma—how could I train with them if I wasn't allowed to practice when they practiced? On a whim, I took a chance and asked Reed Sensei if I could join the advanced class before earning the elusive and coveted black belt. To my surprise, he didn't say no, but rather, "I'll think about it."

For five long weeks, he thought about it. Talk about keeping me on standby or in a holding pattern! He finally agreed to let me watch a few classes first without participating. He wanted to see if I could make it there and back from school in time and still have the full hour to train. Our dojo was not within walking distance of school. To get there, I certainly put my newly acquired driver's license, and recently purchased $500, poop-colored Chevy Chevette to the test.

This car was nothing to write home about. The memory of rolling up in it for a first date still makes me cringe. Looks aside, the car did get me from point A to point B and back relatively inexpensively, safely, and on time. On the super-bright side, my poop mobile also got me out of eating at the exceptionally bad high school cafeteria, which I replaced with Taco Bell. Today, the thought of consuming six to eight fifty-nine cent bean burritos makes me sick and transports me transports me to the early 1990s.

Once Reed Sensei saw I could successfully make it to class and back, he agreed to let me begin training in the advanced class. The agreement, however, came with two stipulations: 1) I would keep my grades up, and 2) I would still have enough energy left over to meet the physical requirements of the night class. He could also, at any time, if he felt I wasn't keeping up my end of the bargain, forbid me to attend the midday class. I kept my end of the bargain and met his requirements, class after class, and the extra class eventually became part of my daily routine.

A couple of months after joining the advanced class, we were performing front kick after front kick, up and down the length of the mat throughout the hour of class, and Reed Sensei repeatedly told me I was doing it incorrectly. He pointed out my lack of power and speed and said I was landing too hard on the mat.

Everyone else, apparently, had become perfect kicking machines because they all received praise and compliments that day and quite often, I was the only one being corrected, criticized, and humiliated. I became very frustrated because I knew the other students were making many of the same mistakes. Reed Sensei continuously found things wrong with many of my techniques and movements, and he would jump down my throat, telling me what I needed to correct.

I didn't know why he continued to single me out. He might have been in an awful mood on this day more than others, or my technique could have been as bad as he said. I felt lost and clueless. What I knew for certain was the last thing I wanted was to give him a reason to ban me from the class.

That night, before I left for my evening karate session, my mom could see the frustration on my face and asked about my day. To her surprise, I told her it was about karate rather than some melodrama from the soap opera that was my all-American high school. I explained I felt Reed Sensei no longer wanted me in the midday class because I wasn't good enough. This was my own deduction and no one else's.

She asked, "Does he criticize others the way he does you?"

I replied, "No, and when he does correct others, it's never in the same way. He intentionally singles me out. I feel like he's picking on me. I become the example of how not to do it. It embarrasses me and makes me not want to be there anymore."

"I can see why you feel like you're letting him down and he's picking on you," my mom replied. "It's quite possible he thinks you have certain areas you need to improve greatly. However, I think there's a reason you haven't thought about that could be the true source of his severe critique. I'd like you to think outside the box for a moment. Do you think it's possible he's doing that because he believes in you and wants you to succeed more than anyone else in class? Possibly, he has such high standards for you because he sees you have greater potential. Or he thinks, out of everyone there, you're the one who shows the most interest and willingness to learn and improve."

After she posed these questions, reality hit me like I was inside the classic game *Frogger* and had just been struck and flattened out while attempting to cross the road by a nitroglycerin truck moving at high speed. I reflected on times when I'd felt singled out and realized my mom had hit the nail on the head. I was blind, but now I could see. I just needed to look at the situation in a different way, through a different lens. Reed Sensei, as well as my mom, was making a genuine effort by giving me thorough and honest feedback. As a result, I began to see class, Reed Sensei, and my training in an entirely new way!

Sometimes, the best things are truly hidden in plain sight. Finding that gem in all the mud is the secret. Sometimes, we become biased and let our emotions and pride cloud our perception. Once it was brought to my attention, Reed Sensei's reasoning seemed obvious. I felt ridiculous and slightly ashamed for even thinking about quitting the class, and for whining or complaining in the first place.

Being criticized had been tough to handle, especially coming from him, but upon reflection, I realized it was an effective tool for bringing out my natural best.

SELF-REFLECTION

Self-reflection is one of the best ways to shift how you think and discover a better connection to yourself. It gives us an opportunity to challenge how we think and feel, and recognize the things we are worried about are sometimes gems in disguise. Rather than ruminating on the bad things people tell us about our weaknesses or mistakes, it's important to take the time to reflect and think about their intent behind the message.

In the black belt class, the criticism I had experienced was exacerbated by my own emotions. I was taking Reed Sensei's remarks as an expression of disapproval of my faults and mistakes rather than seeing the real intent—to ensure I became better and more successful in training and life in general. I needed to take ownership of my faults, weaknesses, and failures, and check my pride at the door. I had to let go of my stubbornness and accept the lessons Reed Sensei was teaching me. Like my mom proposed, rather than taking it personally and letting it ruin my day, or even worse, quitting, I needed to learn to spin it in a positive way.

Being defensive about our shortcomings can be dangerous because it allows our egos to be wounded and can create resentment. It can cause us to lash out and thus run the risk of missing out on something important that could truly improve our future. Using criticism to our advantage by applying it to learn more about ourselves and how we handle challenging situations increases our ability to improve as a student, leader, and mentor.

Even when we know constructive criticism is good for us, it may be difficult to accept and improve what we are shown. In the end, the only way we can get better is to accept that we all have weaknesses and faults, learn from and accept them, and do something positive with the criticism. It is important to remember that criticism is only constructive if the one delivering it intends it to be, and then one builds something with it. Otherwise, it is simply criticism!

MENTOR/MENTEE

John Stewart started as a stand-up comedian and eventually branched out into acting, producing, writing, and hosting *The Daily Show* for sixteen years. Pushing the envelope of comedy and speaking from his heart about controversial topics didn't come without a barrage of criticism. Stewart often credits the late George Carlin as his mentor, not only because Carlin is widely regarded as one of the most influential American stand-up comics of all time, but because he was a pioneer in political and cultural satire and weathered the storm of public criticism with panache. Stewart has expressed gratitude for Carlin's great influence and mentorship.

SUMMARY

Constructive criticism can't be considered an insult, a reflection of your self-worth, or an attack on who you truly are. It's just someone's observation. Although it's a challenge to accept and learn from it, we know it's worth listening to if the intentions are good. It needs to be well thought out, objective, and come from good intentions. Feedback is crucial fuel to move you forward and help you achieve greater success.

ACTION STEPS

THINK

How do you handle or react to criticism? Can you name a time it made you quit or want to quit something?

_____

_____

Is there a way you'd appreciate being critiqued or positively criticized? Think of what your "sum of 4" would be for receiving positive criticism.

_____

_____

List four people you would willingly accept any feedback or criticism from and have no problem with what they said. If this is too hard, shorten the list to two!

_____

_____

_____

_____

DO

Realize that constructive criticism can provide important insight into your weaknesses. We are all fallible; we all make mistakes or need improvement. Sometimes an outside perspective can bring to light what we never saw before. Take it seriously and use this knowledge to improve and learn. The message should be forward thinking to help you avoid pitfalls and mistakes, not backward, telling you what you did wrong.

Ignore those who hate, envy, are threatened by, or are angry with you. Learn to differentiate the kinds of critics speaking to you. Take what is left, which is constructive criticism, and grow and learn from it.

4

MENTOR • DEVELOP • **EXECUTE** • SUCCEED

CHAPTER 13
LEVERAGING INFLUENCE

"Human behavior flows from three main sources: desire, emotion, and knowledge."

— Plato

Using constructive criticism is one of the most effective ways to improve and change your life. We saw in the last chapter that instead of seeing someone's critique or feedback as mean or cruel, we can use it to our advantage. By not taking what people say personally, and sifting through the message, we can truly learn from others' observations about us.

As you may have noticed, every chapter intentionally begins with a famous quote that is relatable and intended to influence you to better all aspects of your life. The quotes remind me of the inspirational sayings on posters with picturesque landscapes on the walls of school counselors and doctors' offices. As a kid, even though they were just words on pictures, these messages influenced me to be more positive, just like the inspirational quotes in each chapter of this book are intended to do for you.

This chapter will help identify specifically how our influence, like that of posters and quotes, can inspire and persuade others to act and change their behavior. We'll focus on persuading and influencing for the improvement and betterment of ourselves, plus our mentees, students, family members, friends, coworkers, employees, and communities. We do this knowing that winning someone over to our way of thinking will empower us and enhance our connection to that person.

Think of all the people who have influenced you, inspired you, and persuaded you to reach higher and improve yourself. Have you ever changed your behavior or acted a certain way because of what someone said, did, or asked? Do you know why you were willing to make this change for them? Maybe it was because of your trust and confidence in them.

THE ART OF PERSUASION

Being able to persuade others is raw power. For good or bad, it can move people to do what you want them to do. Persuasive people can get someone to use drugs, buy them things, start a fight, or ruin their lives. A persuasive person can also keep people from using drugs, not waste their money, avoid a fight, or reach for greatness.

An effective mentor and great leader can persuade without force, manipulation, intimidation, or control. They naturally gain the respect, love, admiration, trust, and empathy of others who wish to emulate them. One of the world's most popular motivational speakers, Zig Ziglar, once said, "The most important persuasion tool you have in your entire arsenal is integrity."

The process of changing another's attitudes, beliefs, or behaviors through voluntary compliance takes knowledge, authority, trust, and credibility. You must be authentic and true to who you are. Those who model the behavior others wish to emulate have the most effective influence. Persuasion is a powerful vehicle for significant change, but applying persuasive tactics doesn't guarantee success. Like John Heywood's proverb collection of 1546 said, "You can lead a horse to water, but you cannot make it drink."

In other words, even though we can create a favorable and easy circumstance for others, in the end, we can't force them to do anything. Even when someone knows it's the right thing to do, or even to survive, they will only do it if they so choose. As a personal trainer of seventeen years with well over 30,000 hours of training others, I've experienced this aversion to making healthier choices time and time again.

It can be very frustrating as a personal trainer or strength coach to see a client ignore your expert advice on how to live a healthier and stronger life. Even when they know in their hearts they should follow the advice, it is difficult to influence someone long-term if they are not ready to make a major change.

Ultimately, it's up to each individual to drink the water. Even with fact-based knowledge and research, human reasoning can be flawed. Whether it's changing spending habits, behavior, attitude, or health and wellness choices, it's up to each of us to make our own decisions. We must have the desire to change, using a specific purpose or goal to move ahead. As American actress and former fashion model Sharon Stone once said, "People don't change their behavior unless it makes a difference for them to do so."

In my experience, even the most influential people have difficulty persuading others to do something they don't really want to do. Effectively communicating and proving the new way is better is not an easy task. But it's not hopeless. Even with human nature's limitations, an inspirational leader or mentor can turn the tide and reach their audience.

To have a positive influence takes true discipline, determination, passion, and dedication. Leading by example, no matter the profession, can motivate others to develop their skills, improve, and change their lives. By practicing what we preach and never expecting someone to do something we aren't willing to do ourselves, we gain the respect, admiration, and trust of others. This is the surest recipe for effectively influencing others to do difficult or even terrifying things. Leaders and mentors who master the power of influence capture the strategies that best help sculpt the actions, behaviors, and opinions of others in any situation.

FINDING MY CURRENCY

In general, the term currency refers to a system of money used in a country to pay for goods and services. From a parent's perspective, a child's currency is basically something they value. It could be a toy, an activity, a special treat, or screen time. Every child, like every adult, has their own currency. By identifying their currency, you can leverage it.

Once you know what a child values, you can use it as either a punishment or a reward. If they do something great, they are rewarded with that currency. If they behave badly, you can take it away. For example, my daughter loves cartoons. If she misbehaves, throws tantrums, or refuses to listen, we take away her screen time for the day or until she improves her attitude.

After reading Gary Chapman's *The 5 Love Languages*, I realized that being accepted by my teachers in school was my love language and had been important to me. I yearned for my teachers' approval and praise. At that time, a simple hug showed me they were proud of and accepted me. Times have changed, but teachers who show pride in their students can still instill the belief in them that they're good people.

What I wanted most was Reed Sensei's approval, and I would do anything to earn and keep it. This meant always respecting him, playing by his rules, doing my best, and never letting him down or embarrassing him. I found that following his example and always giving 100 percent was the surest path to achieving the admiration and acceptance I was looking for. Training at the dojo with him also happened to be what I valued most. It was my currency!

A MOTHER'S HAIL MARY

Did your mom ever say to you, "Just wait until your father comes home!"? Because my parents divorced, this threat didn't work for me. My mom could threaten me for stepping out of line, but she wasn't very intimidating.

As I grew older, I got a little too big for my britches and defied her at every turn. I rebelled, misbehaved, and said things no teenage boy should ever say to his parents. I was angry, upset, and bitter about my parents' divorce.

In hindsight, I naively blamed, judged, and severely punished my mom for their divorce by taking it out on her. I was cruel to the woman who not only took care of me but sheltered me from the reasons for their split. Today, I feel sheepish having held her responsible for the divorce before knowing all the facts—it wasn't her first choice nor her doing. In retrospect, I respect her more now for taking the blame and never speaking ill of my dad. She left it up to me, as I became an adult, to form my own opinion of my father's behavior and lifestyle.

At the time, however, I apparently thought my acting like the Antichrist in the movie *Damien* was justified. I certainly knew how to push my mom's buttons and didn't think twice about doing so. One morning before school, I overstepped my boundaries with some disrespectful remark because she threatened to kick me out of the house permanently. Thinking it was a hollow attempt to scare or threaten me, I left for school unafraid, smirking as I walked out the door and thinking, *Whatever.*

After school that day, I could hardly wait to get to the dojo to train. As I approached the main entrance, I could see through the windows that I was not the first to arrive. A woman with long dark hair was sitting with her back to the window and speaking to Reed Sensei. As I bowed and entered the front door, both Reed Sensei and the guest stopped talking, which was when I noticed the guest was my mom! I knew in an instant the reason for her unusual visit.

At that moment, I felt I had to pick my jaw up off the ground because I knew their conversation couldn't be about anything good. Reed Sensei simply looked at me and nodded in the locker room's direction—meaning I should go change and get ready for class. I could feel my stomach drop like a battleship's anchor to the ocean floor as I quickly made my way to the changing room. If I'd had a tail, it would have been between my legs. I couldn't imagine what or how much my mom had divulged, but I knew I was in trouble.

I never took so long to change into my *gi* (uniform). From inside the changing room, I could hear other students arriving. Having stalled as long as possible, I stepped out of the room to find my mom had already left. Even as I type this story, my palms are sweating as I recall the feelings of shame and self-disgust I experienced as I warmed up on the mat.

That class would be the longest, most excruciating ninety minutes I ever experienced. During class, I anticipated the possible outcomes. I didn't want class to end because that meant dealing with the inevitable—regretting my actions toward my mother!

The anticipation was eating me from the inside. I was terrified because I knew I was inexcusably in the wrong. Reed Sensei held substantial influence and power over me. Someone I feared letting down would be deciding my punishment.

Class was pretty normal, but as it neared its end, the butterflies in my stomach became more and more active. When class finally ended, the butterflies partied like rock stars, sending me off to pray to the porcelain god and offer up my most recent school lunch.

After wiping the lunch off my face and cleaning the toilet lid, I folded my uniform at the pace of a sloth to ensure I'd be last to leave. Reed Sensei's non-verbal communication was enough to inform me I needed to stay after class. In fact, he played it cool the entire class. No one had an inkling I was about to receive the talk of my life. I just hoped it wouldn't be the end my life!

Head down, tail between my legs, and hands cradling my gym bag like a stuffed animal, I sat in a chair right next to him. He told me to look directly in his eyes and listen intently because he would only say this once. Shivering uncontrollably and with tears already forming in my eyes, I forced my eyes to meet his and listened to him say, "Blue, you will *never* speak to your mom this way again.

And you will never treat her this way again. Because if I hear that you do, you will never again be allowed to set foot in this dojo. Do you understand me?"

As my shoulders trembled and tears rolled down my cheeks, I replied with a very affirmative, "Yes, Sensei."

Then it was over, as if nothing had happened. I took my gym bag and bowed, leaving the dojo. That was the true power of influence. He didn't have to lift a finger or say anything else. He knew I understood him and that I'd beaten myself up internally the entire class—that I had already thoroughly punished myself. My anxiety and anticipation of the unknown had been a peerless punishment. Often, not knowing is worse and more powerful than knowing.

The choice Reed Sensei offered me—basically shape up or ship out—left the ball in my court. Of course, I decided before my butt left the chair. On my way home, eager to apologize and grovel to my mom for her forgiveness, I had two major epiphanies.

First, my mom not only deserved greater respect and appreciation as my mom, but she had the strategic mind of a four-star general! To this day, I still compliment her on how she handled the situation by asking for Reed Sensei's help. It was a mother's desperate Hail Mary pass to realign her son's behavior, and it proved successful. She had successfully identified her teenage son's "currency"—what I valued most. For other kids in the '90s, the currency might have been time with their girlfriend or boyfriend, their car, money, or a Nintendo Game Boy, but for me, it was time with Reed Sensei and our dojo. Well played, Mom. Checkmate.

Second, I discovered the true meaning of influence. Reed Sensei had me wrapped around a single finger, tearfully trembling like a lost kitten. This man's acceptance and approval was more important to me than any selfless act. At that moment, I realized the depth of my respect, love, and admiration for Reed Sensei and the real power and influence a mentor can have.

My training resumed the next morning with a new attitude on life, martial arts, and certainly, toward my mom. From that point on, I treated her with the utmost respect, which she deserved, and I vowed never to put Reed Sensei in that position again. There would be no second chance. This was the rawest meaning of the power of influence—not to be confused, of course, with "The power of the dark side."

MENTOR/MENTEE

Arnold Schwarzenegger loved, cherished, admired, and respected Joe Weider and called him his father figure and key mentor. Weider had helped popularize bodybuilding worldwide, including founding the Olympia bodybuilding competitions. He saw the potential in Schwarzenegger. Weider always gave Schwarzenegger his time, energy, money, and advice on training, and he would vouch for him in his business ventures. He understood how to motivate him because he knew Schwarzenegger's currency: he wanted to be legendary. Weider helped inspire Schwarzenegger and his fame skyrocketed, branching out well beyond just being a bodybuilder. Weider once said, "Every sport needs a hero, and I knew that Arnold was the right man."

SUMMARY

The way we act reflects who we are. If we act sloppily, then we are sloppy inside. If we're late, act like a jerk, or whatever, it's because we're that inside. Sometimes, our greatest battle is with our own actions, and the choices we make become a reflection of who we are on the inside. A positive influence, someone we truly admire and respect, easily has the power to change our behaviors, opinions, and actions so we can be our best.

A strong leader or mentor who knows what their mentee's currency is can successfully get them to move mountains. The power of influence provides ample opportunities, strategies, and lessons to instill character and strong values in another and help them achieve greatness.

ACTION STEPS

THINK

What is it you value most or is your currency? It could be a person, place, or thing.

___

___

___

Do you know what your loved ones value most? Or what your friends or colleagues value most?

___

___

___

How can you use that knowledge to positively influence them?

_____

_____

_____

Who, among all those in your life, has true power to positively influence you? Who matters most? Who would you be embarrassed to let down or disappoint?

_____

_____

_____

DO

Walk the walk and talk the talk. Think before acting because your actions and words can define you and reflect who you truly are.

Call the most influential people in your life to ask them if they know what your currency is. You might be surprised by what they say.

Voice your values to your loved ones, your boss, managers, or corporate heads so they can better understand what moves you and use it to bring out your best.

Ask the people in your life what their currency is if you don't already know. Use this knowledge to better relate to and create stronger relationships with them.

4

MENTOR · DEVELOP · **EXECUTE** · SUCCEED

CHAPTER 14
ADOPTING A GROWTH MINDSET

"Intellectual growth should commence at birth and only cease at death."

— Albert Einstein

In the last chapter, we acknowledged that a strong and inspirational mentor or leader can positively alter someone's way of thinking, acting, and reacting. Understanding what a person truly values allows another to influence them to do more than they thought they could possibly do. Understanding what motivates us is critical for a mentor in successfully guiding us.

Now, we'll look at how continuous learning and growth are imperative not only to expanding our personal motivation, but to our very identity and existence. Lifelong learning and self-growth are crucial to living successful and fulfilling lives.

Do you enjoy challenging your mind and learning new things? Or do you baulk at the idea of learning new things because you feel safe and content where you are? Maybe you feel like your life or career has become stagnant, that you've settled, become complacent, or lost some kind of competitive advantage. Whatever your current feelings, to improve yourself and unlock your greatest potential, you have to be willing to continue to grow your entire life.

A SINKING SHARK

To live life without continuous learning is unthinkable. Globalization and rapidly evolving technologies are reasons we must maximize our ability to learn. Otherwise, we run the risk of becoming obsolete. One of the best things about life is we never have to stop learning. We can't know everything, we can't learn everything, or be the master of everything, but learning is the foundation of continuous improvement, innovation, and success. As Indian philosopher, author, and speaker Jiddu Krishnamurti once said, "There is no end to education. It is not that you read a book, pass an examination, and finish with education. The whole of life, from the moment you are born to the moment you die, is a process of learning."

You can always acquire or improve some skill or find a new talent to adopt. Whether you are a child, teenager, or adult, and no matter your personal or professional roles, the acquisition of knowledge is always at your fingertips, allowing for further growth and success.

If you ever catch yourself thinking there's nothing else to learn, then you're not being honest with yourself or looking hard enough. There are always new technologies, ideas, responsibilities, and opportunities to explore. The art of standing still and becoming complacent should never be practiced. Every moment you're standing still, someone is passing you by, and you're getting farther and farther behind. American actor Brad Pitt hit it home by saying, "By nature, I keep moving, man. My theory is, be the shark. You've just got to keep moving. You can't stop."

The world's most successful people understand they must continuously learn to be successful. Otherwise, their capabilities diminish and their importance wanes. Acquiring new knowledge and competencies not only expands your skills but helps you develop future opportunities. These, in turn, make you more successful and competitive, and they help you grow personally and professionally.

It's up to you. You can be open-minded and continue to learn and grow or you can watch learning opportunities pass by as you become complacent and less relevant.

SELF-GROWTH

Adopting a growth mindset and lifelong learning means continuously diving into something new. We can develop new skills through effort and practice, but it takes breaking out of our comfort zone. Our mind truly is our most powerful and valuable asset—we just have to *choose* to use it.

Curiosity about the unknown drives learning. A sense of wonder, a desire to know, offers the opportunity to grow, see new things, and seek new adventures. A lack of confidence, lack of courage, or hesitation can also keep us from moving forward and put us in a mental cage. It comes down to asking ourselves if we want to grow and whether we are willing to emerge from complacency. Our mind can either maintain the status quo or it can take action, seize the day, and transform our lives.

You must be willing to stimulate your mind and kick your personal life and career into overdrive. You need to go back to school, literally and figuratively. See the world as your classroom and everyone in it as an influential teacher. You'll have to invest personal time and money in developing your mind, but it is more than worth the effort and expense.

Our willingness to learn and our ability to use our imagination affords us limitless possibilities for chasing and capturing our dreams. A wealth of knowledge is available to us, so no matter our background, it's up to us to scour the earth to fulfill this thirst for knowledge. A love of learning can be developed, or it can be an innate desire that burns from the inside. Often, we can find this enthusiasm and be motivated to learn by a simple introduction to something of interest.

THE CHALLENGE

My dad loved to read, especially newspapers and science fiction. His affection for reading was so great that he would purchase entire stocks of books from bookstores going out of business. He would buy them by the box or pallet to stock his personal library in our home.

The library was a 1,000-square foot room filled corner to corner with ten-foot-high shelves, full of alphabetically organized books. As a kid, my aversion to books, as well as my respect for my dad's organizational skills, kept me from ever reading anything on the shelves. However, what did attract me to his library, or man cave, was the miniature electric train set and track he had placed above the bookshelves that ran the entire span of the room. I would detach myself from reality for hours playing with the model set while he was engrossed in reading.

Although my education was important to my parents, even after their divorce, I never showed much interest in anything scholastic, other than martial arts topics. And although there was a giant library accompanied by a cool train set at my fingertips as a kid, there were zero books on how to train like a ninja, so I never grew to appreciate other books or my dad's collection.

Reed Sensei also had a library, but it failed by comparison, regarding size and material. It was a tiny shelf behind his desk with fewer than 100 books. Among the students and other instructors, they were known as the forbidden fruit, being restricted and requiring top secret clearance. We are talking Area 51 security over his library.

There were books about all things: karate, judo, aikido, stretching, fighting, competition, tactics, technique, and martial arts. Many of the books included articles on Reed Sensei himself, his background, and his worldwide influence on martial arts. The only thing missing was a video library full of low-budget ninja movies. Hanging on the wall directly above the books was a mysterious, well-used machete with military paracord wrapped around the grip. To this day, I do not know its history or why it was there, other than to protect the books, but every student had their own theory.

We kept our hands off the forbidden fruit, even though I personally yearned to read them all. Remember, these were pre-Amazon days and chain bookstores didn't offer many of these titles. Many were originals written by Reed Sensei's instructors in Japan, or his friends and colleagues. Even today, you would be hard pressed to find many of those rare titles.

One night, after class, I sat alone with Reed Sensei by his desk and his infamous bookshelf. After putting on my shoes and packing my uniform in my super-cool Darth Vader *Star Wars* backpack ("*Jansport* backpacks take a hike"), he said, "It has come to my attention that you aren't interested in reading anything in or outside of school. Is that so?"

Even as a freshman in high school, I wondered if one of my parents had thrown me under the bus again. After I gave him a roundabout answer, he replied, "I have a proposal to make."

I had no idea what he meant, but I listened as he explained, "I'm going to make you an offer. I think I know why you don't like reading, and I'd like an opportunity to fix that. Therefore, I propose a challenge for you. If you read a book I suggest, cover to cover, I will let you choose any book on the shelf behind me to read. And, if you complete this challenge successfully, I am willing to bet once again that you will take me up on the challenge to follow that."

My interest successfully piqued, I asked what he meant by another challenge.

"I'll bet," he replied, "that you'll enjoy the books [notice the plural] that I propose so much that you'll continue the cycle over and over. All for the simple price of choosing another book to read from behind me. I'm so certain this challenge will turn you into a reader, and on topics other than martial arts, that I'm willing to offer you to keep any book behind me if I'm wrong."

My jaw dropped, not because he knew I'd take any challenge he proposed, but because I would get to choose *any* book from the forbidden tree! And that I could keep a piece of the fruit made it a totally sweet deal. He knew my currency for sure. I eagerly accepted the challenge, just thinking, *God, please don't let the initial book be the Bible!*

MY OWN LIBRARY

The first book, for a kid who hated to read, was a lengthy 300-plus-page book by Louis L'Amour called, *Last of the Breed*. It tells the fictional story of a Native American United States Air Force pilot, who's a survivalist and self-defense instructor. He gets shot down by the Soviets over the ocean between Russia and Alaska and is then captured. He has one night to escape from a Siberian prison and make it to the Bering Strait. The book chronicles his use of the skills he learned as a child from his elders to survive, evading the Russian military and a Yakut Indian the Russians employ to track him down.

What young boy who grew up with action movies of the '80s wouldn't love this? This, and the fact that the story was similar to Reed Sensei's life in the Air Force as the head of a survival school, and master in several martial arts, let him know in advance that his challenge was a sure win and I wouldn't be keeping one of his books.

I couldn't put the book down. I read page after page, finishing it in less than a day. For the first time in my life, I truly enjoyed reading. It allowed me to travel to different parts of the world, through someone else's eyes. Hours went by as I lost all track of time and left reality. I don't think I even remember eating that day. I felt like the boy in *The NeverEnding Story* who was actually part of the story being told.

True to his word, after I finished *Last of the Breed*, Reed Sensei allowed me to choose a book from his forbidden tree. We continued this book for book challenge for two years, until I had read most of the books on his shelf. This lesson taught me reading books outside my comfort zone allows me to open my horizons and learn about anything and everything. I learned there is no limit to things to learn, places to visit, or adventures to take—all from reading. Reading became an exercise for my mind, just as training had for my body.

Just like a cherished mentor's opinion, reading is powerful and can influence us. Learning and reading make you question and challenge things you may have believed your entire life. No matter your age, books can open your eyes to things you never considered before. Former First Lady Laura Bush once said, "Libraries allow children to ask questions about the world and find the answers. And the wonderful thing is that once a child learns to use a library, the doors to learning are always open."

Reed Sensei's library and his challenge opened the door for my interest and love for foreign languages, cultures, travel, and history. This was when I learned the importance of nutrition, having an active lifestyle, stretching, and everything known about martial arts. I learned the importance of saving money, budgeting, bookkeeping, and I learned how to start a legitimate business—not just selling sports cards out of my school locker—and an understanding of financial freedom.

I also learned knowledge is not only powerful but easily accessible to everyone. You don't need to physically keep going to school well after college, but you must continue applying yourself as if you are always in a classroom surrounded by teachers. American zookeeper and TV personality Jack Hanna said, "The world is the true classroom. The most rewarding and important type of learning is through experience, seeing something with our own eyes."

Do you look at life as a chance to constantly learn and grow your mind? Reed Sensei helped me understand the quote above at an early age. He taught me the importance of finding topics that interested me. I learned something new doesn't have to be scary or impossible. Even if something is difficult or challenging, learning can be fun and can come from an array of different platforms. He taught me that knowledge is power, and we are never too old to learn new talents and skills or have new experiences.

Many years later, after Reed Sensei's death, I still feel honored to be given the opportunity to select and acquire most of the books from his collection of forbidden fruit. These treasures now reside in my own library and are waiting for my daughter to discover one day.

MENTOR/MENTEE

Napoleon Hill was an American self-help guru and author who credited Andrew Carnegie with inspiring him to write one of the all-time best-selling self-help books, *Think and Grow Rich*. Hill said Carnegie planted in him the seed to write about what Hill had been teaching for years. Although many people question whether Hill ever met Carnegie, Hill still studied and learned from Carnegie's books and those by other extremely wealthy men how to improve one's life and grow one's wealth.

SUMMARY

It's time to put your mind to work. There are no limits and no excuses for not taking advantage of the wealth of knowledge available to everyone. Always be curious with a desire to learn continuously and explore. Knowledge is abundant, and if you are inquisitive and sincere, there will always be people who will help and support you on your journey. No matter where you are, continuing to learn and grow is the ultimate fast pass to the front of the line.

Everyone has something to teach, and the world can be your university. Keep the momentum going by reflecting on and experimenting with new things. The more you experience, and the more subjects you learn about, the more prepared you become to handle all life's situations. Seeking this knowledge and these valuable skills will make you an asset and help catapult your personal growth and career.

ACTION STEPS

THINK

List your three favorite books and why they are your favorites.

_____

_____

_____

List by name three of your favorite teachers, mentors, or coaches and why they are your favorites.

_____

_____

_____

Think about the things that interest you most and that you'd be willing to prioritize to spend time learning about. Now list your three favorites.

_____

_____

_____

List one thing you can start learning about or researching today. Then list one more thing, each for a one-month, three-month, and one-year goal to learning your four new things. Start studying, beginning to master one of those four things right now. Constantly check your timeline to see if you're ahead of schedule. If so, it's time to add to your list.

Today _____

One-Month _____

Three-Month _____

One-Year _____

DO

Learning should be part of your daily routine. Experiment! Try new things. Keep the momentum going. Continuously strive to learn and keep reflecting.

Whatever you intend to learn, set personal development goals for yourself, and master the basic principles.

Get in the habit of reading books about things you love, don't love, and know nothing about. Explore the library or download the best sellers to your hand-held device. Ask your closest friends what books they enjoy, and then go read them! Join a book club. Whatever you intend to learn or study, set personal development goals for yourself that are realistic. Then master the basic principles to those goals.

Build a diverse network of people from different backgrounds, cultures, ages, and careers to learn from.

Watch tutorial videos on YouTube or listen to podcasts.

Go back to school, learn a new subject, or get certified in something that will help your career.

4

MENTOR · DEVELOP · **EXECUTE** · SUCCEED

CHAPTER 15
NEVER QUITTING

> "The one thing you've gotta do is that you need to always do the best you can do, no matter what the given situation, no matter what comes up against you. You do the best you can do, and you never give up. Never quit."
>
> — James Corden

The last chapter's focus was the need to be on a constant quest to grow as an individual and continuously learn. Never standing still and becoming complacent, but rather constantly, trying to improve and challenge yourself is the surest way to achieve great success. Your mind and the knowledge you gain are your most valuable assets. Never stop learning or trying to gain a competitive advantage.

After acquiring an affection for growing my mind, I was inspired to read books on self-help, motivation, and entrepreneurship. Those books were mostly about people who struggled for years on their roads to success, which were never straight lines. They endured rejection and failure after failure, and yet continued their fight forward. They honed their skills and chased their dreams no matter what obstacles they faced. In the end, what ultimately guaranteed their success was their choice to be resilient, to persevere, and to never quit despite all the odds!

To get started, think about what it means to never give up. Seeing through something difficult, time-consuming, or challenging until the very end is no small feat. Quitting, as well as rationalizing or justifying throwing in the towel before something is completed, is much easier. How does giving up like that make you feel internally after you've stopped? And vice versa, what about how you felt when you chose to persevere and not quit? Were you stronger in the end, and did you feel a deeper pride and satisfaction because you chose not to quit? With those thoughts in mind, let's explore this topic in more detail.

PERSEVERANCE

The temptation to give up is common, and no one's exempt. As we concluded earlier, failure isn't something many of us handle easily or gracefully. And even though we know failure is a common human condition, we're still stunned when it happens. What we can't let become normal, or make routine, is the act of quitting. Instead, our norm should be to stay committed and determined to complete or master the task at hand. Not giving up takes self-belief and perseverance! There is nothing you cannot accomplish if you have faith in your own abilities and work hard. You must believe deep in your heart and in your mind that you are capable of persevering.

Banish self-doubt. Throw it down the garbage shoot. No matter how unobtainable your goals may seem, or how difficult the challenges you face, know that you can overcome. Putting one foot in front of the other, with full determination and the grit to endure, is what it means to persevere. In Superman's words, or at least the guy who played him on television, Dean Cain, "Always believe in yourself and keep going. You don't have to have the most talent in the world. You don't have to be the smartest person in the world. If you persist and you persist and you persist, you will be successful."

Once you commit to a certain path and begin following it, you must do something every day and every minute to move forward until you succeed. Whether it's something as simple as eating a nutritious breakfast every morning to meet a fitness goal, or taking your start-up company public, the size or importance doesn't matter—as long as you are moving in the direction of your long-term goal.

Developing the discipline and attitude to finish what you start and putting that practice into action is the next step.

For example, setting a New Year's resolution to join a gym and get in better physical shape. Working in the fitness industry for nearly two decades, I have seen more than a handful of people start off strong in January, only to disappear or fall off the wagon by February. Sometimes the hardest part is just starting and getting to the gym. You can't finish what you don't start, right? Therefore, paying for a membership, or even putting on your workout clothes right when you wake up or after work, can get you started in taking those small steps toward your goal. Even if the scale isn't moving in the direction you want or the amount of weight per lift isn't going up, finishing rather than abandoning what we start is the path to success.

PATH TO THE DARK SIDE

Whether it's visualizing the finish line in a marathon, or digging deeper for the last sprint in spin class, you must have the willpower to finish the task at hand. It's imperative to keep a clear vision in sight and not allow your mind to wander. Giving up by taking the easy path, or not believing you can succeed, must never enter your mind. As Master Yoda once told Luke, "Always with you what cannot be done. Hear you nothing that I say? You must unlearn what you have learned.... Try not. Do. Or do not. There is no try."

Mentally or physically, you can choose to quit or you can choose to give 100 percent. Both are your choice! I can recall many hour-long, physically taxing classes at the dojo where I'd nearly pass out from exhaustion. But no matter how difficult the class was, I would just have to picture Reed Sensei or hear his voice in my head telling me to dig a little deeper. It's about believing so strongly in yourself and what you are doing, that you refuse to quit.

Every time in class I would find that second wind, just enough in my reserves to persevere. And every time I finished, I'd feel great pride that I had stuck it out. During these intense workouts, I came to understand the mental endurance and persistence required to accomplish anything. I realized it was as simple as just trying. It is about taking small steps forward, giving your absolute best, never allowing self-doubt to enter your mind, and never stopping until you are done.

As a result of this experience and newfound mindset, from that day on, I would not allow myself, mentally or physically, to quit. And, after successfully accomplishing any such given task or routine, I also know that in the future, I will have the resilience to bounce back for more.

RUBBER BAND RESILIENCE

Resilience is similar to perseverance in that it requires a positive mindset to succeed when confronted with a challenge. Resilience is the ability to get better, stronger, healthier, and become more successful after something bad happens. A rubber band, after being stretched, is an example of resilience because of its elasticity and ability to return quickly to its normal state.

We all face different adversities, and some are more difficult to rebound from. Humans are not rubber bands, nor are all problems short-term, but by being resilient, we have the capacity to eventually recover from these adversities, disappointments, and stresses.

One of the most difficult challenges I've ever faced was recovering from a dislocated knee when I was fifteen. While sparring in a *judo* match, not only did I blow out my knee, but I successfully broke off the lateral condoyle to my femur bone. I spent years rehabilitating my knee and underwent six surgeries so I could continue my martial arts training and walk normally.

In the end, I truly gained an appreciation for the human body's ability to recover, the importance of training our weakest points, and the mental resilience it takes to overcome any setback. As a result, I was able to continue my martial arts career, compete competitively worldwide, and successfully translate my misfortunes and experiences into inspiring stories to motivate audiences and thousands of clients. Freelance author Steve Goodier once wrote:

> My scars remind me that I did indeed survive my deepest wounds. That in itself is an accomplishment. And they bring to mind something else, too. They remind me that the damage life has inflicted on me has, in many places, left me stronger and more resilient. What hurt me in the past has actually made me better equipped to face the present.

Setbacks, stress, failure, and disappointments are good for you.

They hurt and are scary, but they are the best forms of education. They teach us to adapt, realign, and improve ourselves. Quitting is like dropping out of life's school. One misses out on the value of failure—the most important lessons and critical experiences. Understanding that we have all wanted to quit at some point cements the fact that these feelings are a part of life. How we choose to deal with those feelings and whether we press on is what matters most.

FIRST-DEGREE BLACK BELT (SHODAN)

At seventeen, and after many years of wearing an array of colored belts, in a school that tested for rank less often than others, the chance to earn the elusive black belt had finally come! All the dreams inspired by my first judo tournament where I met Reed Sensei, the ninja movies, and the magazines I obsessed over as a kid left me yearning to wear a black belt. And more importantly, Reed Sensei had inspired and motivated me to continue going to class through injury, night after night, year after year, to reach this point.

Excited and proud that this moment had finally come, I invited my closest friends and family members to visit the dojo and watch me wear my brown belt for the last time. It was an opportunity to show my training and what all the years of sweat equity had produced. My enthusiasm bled from my *gi* that evening. I was also excited to celebrate at a local restaurant with my friends, family, classmates, and Reed Sensei after passing the exam.

A handful of students were testing that Friday night for different ranks but only a few for their black belts. Testing was only done twice a year for the rank of *shodan* (first-degree black belt), so I had to pass. I was in tip-top shape, had prepared myself mentally for years, and had specifically been practicing the techniques and movements included on the test for months. No way would I let myself fail this exam. Confidence, baby!

Class was grueling, and you could see the stress on everyone's face in anticipation of the testing about to occur. *Shodan* testing was held at the end of class after the lower ranks tested. As a result, there would be enough time to visualize the entire test and successfully passing it. I just hoped sitting in a kneeling position for nearly an hour wouldn't cause cramping—or paralysis.

When the lower ranks finished, it was time for the brown belts to test for their next rank, the coveted black belt. It was finally within reach, and I was up next. This was the moment I had been preparing for my whole ninja-wannabe life! Fifteen minutes stood between me removing the well-frayed brown belt I wore and replacing it with a new black one.

As I began, every one of my movements finished with the crisp sound of the uniform against my body. The audience could hear the crack of my fist or foot against the pad like a small firecracker. My posture and technique resembled a toy top that fluidly spun. My *kiai* (spirit shout) was loud enough to put any screaming power lifter to shame. And during the sparring part of the exam, I had successfully overwhelmed and outwitted my fellow opponents by striking and scoring points first. I was famished, exhausted, and elated to be done after pouring my entire heart into those fifteen minutes.

Reed Sensei then took a moment to grade my exam by tallying up the points earned or missed. Once he had the totals, he announced that, although it was very close, I had failed to accumulate enough points to pass the exam. Any residual energy or adrenaline I had left immediately drained from my body. The rug had been pulled out from under me so quickly that I felt like I was still hovering in a slow and perpetual fall into an abyss.

I instantly began replaying the entire exam in my head, looking for faults. I couldn't recall a single movement I'd botched. Utterly confused by what had just happened, the harsh reality began to sink in—I had just failed!

Then I began projecting the mental anguish and pain I would experience over the next six months while I waited to be tested again. On Monday, I would go to school and reluctantly have to inform my schoolmates I hadn't passed. Lining up in the same order of rank, while wearing the same belt I'd had for the last several years, wasn't going to be fun either. I wanted to leave immediately and go hide under a rock from utter embarrassment and disappointment.

Still reeling from the test result, the celebratory dinner together was like rubbing salt into the wound. I was happy for my classmates' achievements, but attending that dinner certainly tested my humility. Everyone knew how I felt, but I kept up my positive attitude façade for everyone else's sake. Feeling sick to my stomach, I couldn't wait to go home. I knew, however, that even if I was home, I'd still have to face my failure for many more months until I had the chance to retest and redeem myself.

The weekend allowed me to regain my thoughts and remind myself of the purpose behind my training. It wasn't to become a black belt. And, it wasn't really to become a ninja. It was to improve myself and to enjoy the time in our dojo with my classmates, who had become like family, and with my mentor. This slap in the face gave me the strength to keep striving. As American poet Robert Frost said, "The best way out is always through."

Monday night's class came, and just like in any other class, we executed 850 push-ups and focused on several different techniques. Prior to class, there was no discussion about the test results or, more specifically, how I had been the only one to fail. It was gut-wrenching for me to see those who had graduated to new ranks wearing new belts around their waists.

As class wrapped up, we lined up according to rank and kneeled. Just as we were about to bow, Reed Sensei asked me, "Why are you kneeling in the brown belt line?"

Obviously, it was because I'd failed three nights prior, but he knew that. Therefore, I was perplexed.

"You belong up front, in this line," Reed Sensei said, indicating the row of black belts.

Then he pulled a folded black belt from behind his uniform. The real test hadn't been the exam itself. He had known for months from observing my daily training that I'd pass the physical test. The true test, he determined, was whether I had the foundation, self-respect, attitude, courage, strength, humility, patience, perseverance, and resilience to return to class—even in defeat—with my head high and not quit. That was the ultimate test.

I had finally earned the rank of *shodan*. After years of training and making this goal a major priority, I'd done it. All my sacrifice, commitment, and discipline had brought me to that point. I was relieved, ecstatic, and prouder than a peacock as I wrapped the new belt around my waist. Reed Sensei knew I'd set my sights on this goal the day I realized the meaning of his "learning to fall" comment, nearly a decade before. Even in the face of failure and having to retest later, the end was worth the means.

I could have reacted by giving up that night. Instead, I decided to accept the outcome and improve myself for the next time around. Failure, more than anything else in life, is sure to happen. Dealing with failure by pushing forward, persevering, and being resilient sets the stage for future success. Rather than being the end of the story, it may just be a turning point, where you decide not to give up or take no for an answer. When your dreams mean everything to you and you believe you can succeed, by all means, stay resilient and keep going!

MENTOR/MENTEE

Quincy Jones introduced himself at the age of fourteen to a sixteen-year-old Ray Charles after hearing him play at a club. Jones credits Charles as an early inspiration for his own musical success. He also notes that Charles overcame many challenges, including blindness. He respected Charles's resiliency and perseverance. Charles said of his mentee Jones, "He was just an energetic young kid, and he really loved music. You could tell that he wanted to learn, he wanted to know. And because I was able to show him some things, that made me happy, that's what stirred my heart. I could help this kid."

SUMMARY

Never quitting means you believe in yourself. It's the willingness to accept failure as a part of life that everyone experiences. It means taking that failure and learning a critical skill from it to overcome or adapt to future challenges. It is never compromising your values and self-respect. It is never giving up and having the resilience and perseverance to keep pushing forward and not make excuses to quit. This means eliminating the entire thought of giving up, pulling yourself together, and making the decision to get back on track with your goals and dreams.

ACTION STEPS

THINK

How much do you want to succeed in life, and how hard are you willing to work for your dreams?

_____

_____

Think of a time when you quit something you started. Did you, or do you regret that choice? How did you internalize or rationalize your action?

_____

_____

Now think of two times you were resilient. Include the results of those actions.

_____

_____

List two times you decided to persevere through difficult times or challenges. How did you feel when you finished?

_____

_____

DO

Talk to others who have been through similar situations. Ask for their advice and opinion, and ask if it was worth sticking things out till the end for them.

Things and goals don't always go according to plan. Challenges will come and setbacks will occur, but know that they won't last forever. A typical journey to reaching success and your goals can span many years or even decades.

Determine to make a difference in your life! Commit to following through and exert all effort to achieve your goals, plans, dreams, and visions.

Any time you feel like throwing in the towel, tell yourself you started because it was "worth it"! Set your own pace, but always believe in yourself and be persistent. If you fall, get back up—be the rubber band and become accountable to yourself, or someone else.

PART IV
SUCCEED

4

MENTOR • DEVELOP • EXECUTE • **SUCCEED**

CHAPTER 16
STANDING YOUR GROUND

"To fight and conquer in all our battles is not supreme excellence; supreme excellence consists in breaking the enemy's resistance without fighting."

— Sun Tzu

In this chapter, I will explain why one should never assume or judge a book by its cover. We will also revisit the story of my neighborhood bully and how I eventually dealt with him. Part I of this book introduced you to the story of myself as a young boy meeting the most important figure and key mentor in my life. I described the journey this man took me on, the foundation he helped me build, and the lessons he instilled in me to help me gain the confidence necessary to succeed in life and overcome the fear of a tormenting bully. The second and third parts of the book dove into how to develop your personal formula or system, based on the strategies and life lessons we've discussed, so you can continuously grow and improve.

In this final section, I will come full circle by bringing you to the present day, well after my youthful martial arts days and into my adult life and professional career, to share all that I'd learned and discussed in the first two sections to reach my goals and become a successful life coach, martial arts instructor, personal trainer, entrepreneur, business owner, professional keynote speaker, author, and parent. More importantly, this section will show how you, too, can successfully take life by the horns to unleash your best.

SMALL FISH IN A BIG POND

When I left my small US city to attend college in Seattle, Washington, and then to finish college in Tokyo, Japan, and train at the Japan Karate Association's (JKA) World Headquarters, I quickly realized I was no longer a big fish in a small pond, especially in martial arts talent. The JKA serves not only as the headquarters for a specific type of *Shotokan Karate*, but as the international hub for all subsidiary branches. Consequently, the students and instructors were the world's best and top-ranked practitioners. As a student and member of our collegiate karate team, I had the opportunity to train daily with an amazing conglomerate of talent at the headquarters.

Being in my early twenties, living, working, and training in Japan, I thought I was the coolest and best thing since sliced bread. I was on top of the world as a foreigner who spoke Japanese, held multiple black belt ranks, had won many tournaments and championships, was instructed by world class instructors, and in tip-top physical shape from my daily weight training and exercise regimen. I was ready for any competition or challenge. So, one evening in class, when practicing and competing against a student visiting from England, I thought my win was guaranteed.

Turns out, I wasn't the best. That guy wiped the floor with me multiple times that evening. He was hands-down the quickest, most efficient practitioner I'd ever seen or competed against. He made the sensei of our sister school back home look slow. I did my very best and gave it my all, but he could anticipate every move I tried. After class, while stretching with my newfound victor, I asked how he'd become so fast. Seeing my desire to truly understand, he candidly answered, "Blue, I'm slow, and I am not even exaggerating. Even as the all European Champion and UK champion, I get my bum handed to me all the time. There's always someone better, quicker, meaner, or who wants it more than me. I can't win all the time, but I keep refining my technique with speed drills and practice."

I couldn't believe what I was hearing; this super-cheetah had just said he wasn't the best! And he was a champion in two world classes. I had misjudged my competition, become overconfident, and certainly wasn't the big fish in the small pond I thought I was. I was no longer in Spokane, Washington, with its small pool of martial art talent. As Dorothy told her dog, "Toto, I've got a feeling we're not in Kansas anymore."

This visitor from England reminded me there is always someone better. Someone who's faster, can lift heavier weights, is in better shape, is more popular, gets better grades, makes more money, has more toys, or owns a bigger house. As American writer Thom Jones said, "There's always someone bigger and badder than yourself."

This is an absolute truth. This champion also reminded me there is always something to learn from a supportive person with greater experience who is willing to listen without judgment and provide answers and advice. It takes a lot of emotional confidence to come to terms with these facts and realize life should be about collaboration. Your weaknesses are another's strengths and vice versa. To work and collaborate with people from different backgrounds, with different talents and skills allows us to learn from each other (toward a common goal).

A competition can be a wonderful learning experience, whether your first, second, or even last. As previously discussed, a life strategy with an enormous payoff is to surround yourself with those who inspire you to bring out your peak performance and full potential. When you see their work and accomplishments, you are inspired to become better yourself and climb the ladder to reach or surpass their level.

AIRPORT BAGGAGE CLAIM

Our society has created a system of hierarchies that contribute to our obsession with competition and singular excellence. Our lives revolve around how we're perceived, either below or above somebody else. As you advance through life, even as a kid vying for playground respect, competition becomes more serious and hierarchies begin to have significant meaning. Someone must come in first. There is, and only ever will be, one first place winner, which means all others come somewhere between second and last.

Obviously, we would all love to be first and win at everything, every time. Reality, however, dictates a different outcome. It's difficult to accept not winning, plain and simple, especially when we are taught from a young age that coming in second or last is for losers only. Take, for example, what Vince Lombardi, one of the best NFL coaches of all time, said, "There is no room for second place. There is only one place in my game, and that is first place. I have finished second twice in my time at Green Bay, and I never want to finish second again."

Although this mindset can be inspirational, it could also be counterproductive because it's futile to assume being the best every time is possible. The secret of those who truly succeed is admitting to themselves that they're winners and successful, not by being first, but because they live unashamed of the areas in which they need improvement. They are also humble enough to admit when they aren't the best or need to develop a new skill.

Several years ago, on the way to shooting a commercial in Boston, Massachusetts, my flight was running seriously late. I took a red-eye flight from the West Coast and arrived with four hours remaining until I had to be on location. Flustered and in a hurry, I knew I'd have to hustle off the plane from row thirty-one, collect my single checked bag, catch a taxi to my hotel, and check in. All this before having to be on set looking refreshed, instead of like a guy who had just stepped off of an overnight flight.

We deplaned at the pace of molasses, and once it was my turn, I dashed out of the Jetway and made my way to baggage claim. I watched anxiously as the luggage slid down the conveyer belt, one piece after another. And, one by one, passengers took their luggage. The belt came to a halt as the last piece of luggage, mine, fell from the top of the belt to the carousel.

After checking in at my hotel and successfully arriving on set, I couldn't help but laugh, knowing someone's luggage, out of everyone onboard, had to be last. The day I needed to be first happened to be the day it was my turn to be last! We all can't be first, but we can learn to accept this fact and become better the next time. As a result, I no longer check bags and I can give Marie Kando a run for her organizing skills when it comes to efficiently packing any kind of luggage.

NO LONGER AFRAID

After finishing college and working in Japan, I visited Spokane for a few days to train with Reed Sensei, before permanently starting my post-college career in Seattle. To my surprise, I wasn't the only visitor that night. The sister school was also in attendance, along with their sensei. Class began, as did our routine sparring matches that in the past had tied my stomach in knots. Eventually, the time came to face the man I had once feared and who'd explained why I was never able to defeat him.

As we sparred, his moves seemed slower, more telegraphed, and easier to anticipate. I could see in advance the technique he was about to use. I not only could successfully deflect his attacks, but I was able to counter them and score. After the round, he winked at me and said, "Whoa! Look who's not afraid anymore."

After training with the best in the world, I no longer looked at him as unbeatable, mean, or ruthless. Instead, I looked at him as someone I wanted to be as good as and whom I could learn from. I saw him as someone who happened to be much better than I was, but who wasn't invincible or flawless. He was just a man, just as Tony Burton famously said in *Rocky IV*, "You see? He's not a machine. He's a man!"

Now I know that's Hollywood, but like Rocky fighting his Russian opponent Drago, I eventually had to accept the prevailing narrative that I wasn't, in fact, doomed. I could win against any seemingly unbeatable opponent if I didn't give up and just tried to develop my skills. I had to learn to use my training in Japan, my past encounters, and defeats to gain the confidence and experience needed to overcome my fears and opponents. Accepting that somewhere out there someone's always better than me, and that I could at any time encounter that person, has taught me to be more receptive, informed, and prepared.

But what happens when you don't have the opportunity to go back and apply what you've learned to overcome a challenge? In such cases, you need to take a chance, think outside the box, and find the confidence to combat and overcome your fear. At age eight, and with no real training, that is what I eventually did with the neighborhood bully.

"TWO MEN ENTER, ONE MAN LEAVES"

Depending on the source, bullying basically can be defined as a repetitive, unwanted, aggressive behavior that involves a real or perceived power imbalance. The bully is one who perceives someone else as vulnerable and uses their power to make threats, intimidate, coerce, spread rumors, exclude, or attack physically or mentally.

I knew the day would eventually come to confront my neighborhood nemesis. I just hoped it would be well after I'd become a Jedi Knight with the power and strength of Captain America. Also, knowing in advance the wisdom of Dr. Orison Swett Marden, the founder of *Success Magazine*, would have helped: "Most of our obstacles would melt away if, instead of cowering before them, we should make up our minds to walk boldly through them."

A few months after beginning judo, at the end of class one day, Reed Sensei and I waited patiently for my parents to pick me up. He must have seen this as an opportune time to discuss remedying an eight-year old's fear of being bullied. Sitting next to him, with my new child-size uniform neatly folded on my lap, I listened intently as he said:

> Coping with fear is like exercise or practicing how to fall—we get better and stronger with practice. Blue, I didn't win every fight when growing up. Nor did I win every competition on my way to the Olympics. As a national competitor, the thought of losing was catastrophic to me. Or so I thought! Truth is, I never experienced most catastrophes because, in the end, they were only in my mind, not reality. The trick is picturing the best outcome and finding a way there, versus the worst. Remember, like you, he's just a boy with the same fears, emotions, and weaknesses. You will win because you're in control of your mind, not him.

Taking all that in was super-intense. Reed Sensei had just poured out a wealth of information in a matter of a minute. He didn't downplay my fear, call me weak, make fun of me, or disregard my concerns. He took me seriously and implored me to take my power back from the bully by realizing, win or lose, I was ultimately in control. Yes, the bully was bigger, older, and physically stronger, but he was still just a young boy like me. It was time to find a way to get him and my fear out of my head.

About a week later, a brotherlike friend from out of town met me at school for a sleepover. We bet what dinner would be and planned what we'd do for the night on our walk back to my house. I was confident that with a trusty sidekick next to me, who would do anything for me, I would be safe from the bully. With both of us needing to urgently use a bathroom, relief rushed over us as we saw my driveway ahead.

To my surprise, as if I were in the sci-fi action thriller, *Predator*, the bully emerged from behind two pine trees, dressed in camouflage like he was part of the tree. He approached us like a heat-seeking missile, never losing eye contact with me, and said, "Today's the day."

Great. I knew he meant it was the day he planned to kill me. I had to prepare myself for punches being thrown. Remember, at this point I was no ninja. I'd merely learned to fall like a champion, not how to battle like one. I'd been introduced to some basic throws and takedowns, but I was still a galaxy far, far away from having acquired any fighting skills. The last thing I wanted to do was show him my falling technique because that would mean I had been hit really hard.

I figured trying to get past him was the best option for my friend and me, but a crowd of kids on their way home from school began surrounding the three of us and cut off any escape. The sharks could smell blood in the water and were greedily expecting a fight. Now I was living a scene in the post-apocalyptic movie, *Mad Max Beyond Thunderdome*, where a crowd watched and cheered for a single winner to emerge from a death match while repetitively yelling, "Two men enter, one-man leaves."

Talk about peer pressure! The bully, hearing the chant to fight and feeling more emboldened, forcefully pushed me several feet back, right into my friend. This caused me to shift my balance so I wouldn't lose my footing on the gravel. This reaction surely saved me from applying my expert falling technique, but it just made the bully angrier that I hadn't fallen.

This was it—the moment to regain control and the power he had stolen. I didn't know what to do next, but whatever I did would determine the direction of this confrontation, and surely, how I'd feel later that evening, or when I returned to school to face the gossip. There would be plenty of time to play Monday morning quarterback, review, and analyze my mistakes later. That is, of course, if I was still around the next day to return!

Everything around me went silent, and time seemed to slow or stand still. I am talking US Congress slow. I could no longer hear the kids chanting for a David versus Goliath death match. My mind was in ultra-concentration mode, with sensory overload as I played out the best-case or triumphant scenario in my mind. *Engage, react, counter, and regain control.*

Taking a deep breath, I imagined myself back in our dojo practicing leg sweeps, back and forth with a partner, with Reed Sensei observing—having fun practicing and under no pressure. Just as a partner had done hundreds of times in class, I pictured the bully grabbing me. I countered by reversing his momentum, shifting his balance, and successfully turning the table on his aggression by sweeping his leg, causing him to slip on the gravel and split his legs apart like a wishbone. His camouflage pants ripped right down the middle louder than his painful scream.

This, at least, was the best scenario I pictured in my mind seconds after he pushed me. Being the clichéd underdog who fights and defeats the big, bad bully is an old story, told many times before. And I would love to tell that story, but what really happened is much different.

As everything went silent, the solution hit me harder than I'd ever fallen or been thrown in class. I realized the way he pushed me wasn't any harder than when I was regularly pushed in class. He was just a boy like me who had the same vulnerabilities. My vulnerability was being shamed by this boy. Therefore, on the spot and with a best friend at my side, I concluded that reversing my vulnerability might remedy the situation. So, while he was a few feet away, I pointed in the direction of my friend behind me, and returned the threat by saying, "If you make another move toward me, we will both pee on you!"

He looked perplexed as he paused to weigh my threat. Especially as my friend and I, with no spoken words, simultaneously moved our hands toward the top of our shorts, primed and ready to pull them down. Disregarding my words, he cautiously approached us with hands in a typical boxing position as the audience chanted. I looked directly at my friend and feverishly nodded in the bully's direction. Even with a crowd of several onlookers, my friend and I pulled our shorts down, revealing all, and took aim.

After successfully hitting our target for a full three to four seconds, the bully, in absolute disbelief and with a urine-soaked chest and face, ran off. The spectators started laughing and pointing at him as he hightailed it home.

Meanwhile, I smiled. I was unashamed and slightly proud of the fact that my friend and I, on the spur of a moment, had just urinated on demand in public on a mean kid. I'd done what I thought was impossible. I had successfully stood my ground, regained control of my fears, and empowered myself without the use of violence. No punches were thrown, and although I weighed a little less, I was still standing intact with all my teeth. As Reed Sensei had promised, I had changed the balance of power in my favor.

Looking back, I see that peeing on the boy was primitive, crude, and probably not the best idea. Even today, I'm slightly embarrassed by my actions, but as an eight-year-old boy, I think it was a brilliant idea and a solid victory. Not long after, the bully's grandmother knocked on our front door and yelled at my mom for what my friend and I had done to her grandson. From behind the door, my friend and I secretly listened to my mom's ultimate comeback. "Wow, that's a real *pisser* your grandson had to learn his lesson that way."

I'm not sure what else my mom said before she closed the front door, but I know the boy never again picked on me or anyone else on the way home from school. No one at my school ever made fun of me either. Apparently, I'd successfully earned street cred and gained the confidence necessary to conquer my fears. I'd misjudged the bully's strength and power, and he had been overconfident and misjudged his victims' ability to improvise, adapt, and overcome. I also realized one should never doubt one's self and abilities, or be over- or under-confident, and that I alone am in control of my fears.

MENTOR/MENTEE

The editor of *French Vogue* introduced Yves St. Laurent to Christian Dior in Paris. As a result, St. Laurent became Dior's personal assistant, where he learned the secret of *haute couture* (exclusive custom-fitted clothing), how to run a business, and everything fashion. St. Laurent aligned himself with someone at the top of their industry who sparked his career, an expert who could teach and mentor him in the ways of becoming successful himself. Later, even though these fashion designers were considered competitors within the industry, if you asked them, they were more like mentors to each other. St. Laurent once said, "Dior fascinated me. I couldn't speak in front of him. He taught me the basis of my art. Whatever was to happen next, I never forgot the years I spent at his side."

SUMMARY

There's always someone who is better or has more than you. Use this fundamental truth to make a better you and take more chances! If someone is better than you, don't be afraid to ask them how they got where they are. You have your own set of qualities and skills that set you apart. Capitalizing on your strengths and surrounding yourself with those who teach you to perform at a higher-level is the ultimate path to growth and success.

In my experience, if you run or walk away from mental or physical confrontations or challenges, you'll continue to be called out, picked on, or bullied. And if you choose the opposite path and fight every person or argue every challenge, you'll end up alone, hurt, or beaten at some point. Giving up isn't the answer either. You must stand your ground by being true to yourself rather than being combative. You have to find a path around, over, underneath, or through the obstacle. In the end, you have the choice to regain your power and take back control of any challenge you encounter. How you decide to confront these challenges will directly determine and shape your future.

ACTION STEPS

THINK

List three people you could ask about how they got to where they are, got what they have, or became so good at what they do.

1. _____
2. _____
3. _____

Now go ask and talk to those three people!

Write down three lessons or skills you have learned throughout your life as a result of not winning or taking first place.

1. _____
2. _____
3. _____

Name a time you've successfully stood up to or taken a stand against an overwhelming or difficult challenge or challenger. How did you feel after standing your ground and maintaining control?

_____

_____

_____

DO

Look at any kind of competition as an opportunity to better yourself, rather than just a chance to win a trophy. Take losing or failing and learn from your mistakes or missteps to better yourself. Find the hidden gem in each experience!

Realize most fears are in your mind and completely manageable—even at first if they seem impossible. Have the courage to stand your ground, regain your power, take control of your thoughts, and be true to yourself.

Find the formula or way around the obstacles and challenges you are bound to face. Remember to think outside the box and be willing to take a chance to step outside it. Sometimes, the solution or result you want isn't always obvious or easy. Continuously ask yourself, "What path or equation can get me to the result I want?"

4

MENTOR • DEVELOP • EXECUTE • **SUCCEED**

CHAPTER 17

EMBRACING CHANGE AND SETTING GOALS

"What if I told you that ten years from now, your life would be exactly the same? I doubt you'd be happy. So, why are you so afraid of change?"

— Karen Salmansohn

In the last chapter, I pointed out the overriding truth that there's always someone who is better than you at something—someone who has more than you, makes more money, has a better job, more fame, or a better life. Even though this is true, just because someone comes in first before you or has more, doesn't mean you can't follow the same path or learn how they became better themselves. Finding someone with qualities you would like to emulate gives you an opportunity to learn a wealth of information from them to develop those qualities in yourself. We also looked at the importance of standing your ground, not misjudging others, and taking control of your fears.

This chapter will focus on reasons we should seek, accept, and embrace change. We'll also emphasize the value and significance of setting and prioritizing goals to map out a roadmap to success.

Being open to the idea of transformation and having a vision of where you want to be will exponentially improve your likelihood of reaching your goals.

Think of the scenario of your future self coming to visit for a meeting or conversation to undergo a difficult but positive and powerful change or realization in your current character or behavior. Are there aspects of your life you'd like to change? Making lists of goals, prioritizing, and setting realistic timelines helps you to embrace these changes and make them easier. When taking small advancements toward your goals, it can make change seem more manageable and ensure you follow through with them until they're achieved.

TRANSFORMATION AND CHANGE

I'm not talking about a werewolf transforming under a full moon, or coins between the sofa cracks. I'm referring to the act of embracing the thrill of actual change to become the next best, upgraded version of yourself. As American author and journalist Gail Sheehy said, "If we don't change, we don't grow. If we don't grow, we aren't really living."

If you are willing to change by going beyond the status quo, you can make significant, long-lasting changes. But if you continue the same old routine and do not embrace change, the cost is living a dull, unfulfilled, and complacent life.

Change and transformation is a natural part of life, but included with the element of fear, many of us reject or resist it because it involves the unknown and leaving our comfort zone. Although it's a scary process, accepting change can be a great thing that betters your life and gets you what you truly desire—a dream life.

Accepting, embracing, and seeking change doesn't come easy, but the sooner you start, the sooner you'll begin to see your life evolve exponentially. Take, for example, learning to type. You may have initially learned to navigate a keyboard with two fingers, like I did. Then I took a high school keyboarding class on the correct way to type, which was to use all ten digits. This meant resisting using the hunt-and-peck method I'd initially taught myself and thought was enough. Frustrated at the thought of regressing before progressing, I fought changing my technique for as long as I could. Soon after, however, I began to see the overwhelming benefits to change, including a rapid increase in words typed per-minute and with less errors.

Today, I'm very thankful I learned the correct and more efficient method of typing. This simple decision truly changed my life, opened opportunities, and created a more valuable me. If I'd been too afraid, stubborn, or unwilling to move outside my comfort zone, I guarantee, I'd still be writing this book and you wouldn't be reading it.

Some people are content to passively coast through their lives, hoping everything comes their way. Others make active choices to understand who they are and what they want. Then they set the goals that will keep them changing, adapting, and moving in the direction they want to go.

Big or small, change is what keeps us alive, shapes us, and moves us up or down. By accepting, appreciating, and implementing change, we make a conscious effort and choice to keep up the fight, grow, move forward, and improve ourselves. It contributes enormously to reaching our goals and achieving greatness. Change is the only means to become the person we want to be. It is our choice whether or not we embrace it. As President Barack Obama noted, "Change will not come if we wait for some other person or some other time. We are the ones we've been waiting for. We are the change that we seek."

REARVIEW MIRROR

Change that can stimulate your personal progress occurs every day, every moment, and every second of your life. Realizing its potential is a crucial part of your personal and career development. It can help you reach your full potential, and like a good book to read, can be your winning ticket out of an unsatisfactory situation.

Even if you don't like change, it is here to stay and is inevitable. It is constant and an integral part of development. Change will not ask for your permission or consent, but there are ways to embrace, control, and use it to your advantage. How you decide to harness the power of change will determine your future. Earlier, I asked if you knew why you were the way you are. Obviously, nature and nurture have played a huge part based on what we've already discussed.

It's important to add that your personal development relies on the transformations and changes you've already experienced that have led you to where and who you are today. Growing by facing the obstacles that life throws at you is a fundamental way of improving yourself. Progress, success, and growth, in other words, can be synonymous with change.

In a world that's constantly changing, wealth, resources, technologies, talents, and trends will evolve with or without you. The ability to contract and expand with life's transformations will ensure a fulfilling and successful life. This, however, will take work and sacrifice down to the simplest aspects of how you act—how you dress or present yourself, whether you take advantage of learning opportunities, or if you surround yourself with an abundance of mentors. As one of baseball's all-time greatest pitchers and Hall of Famer Nolan Ryan said, "Enjoying success requires the ability to adapt. Only by being open to change will you have a true opportunity to get the most from your talent."

If you ever feel your development is too slow—not moving at the speed of a Nolan Ryan pitch —or that you are light years away from reaching your goals, take a moment to look back at where you started. Look in the rearview mirror to see how far you've actually come and the progress you've made. In more ways than one, big and small, you've certainly progressed and grown.

We tend to miss the changes when we look at ourselves directly in the mirror each day. However, if we look at our past, the changes become apparent. As a personal trainer, I've seen many clients lose motivation because they can't see the physical changes soon enough. When I show them where they started, and where they are, using a tape measure or scale, it reminds them of their true physical transformation. A written record of your starting point does wonders to reveal true progress.

Think back to when you were a kid and thought your growth had stalled; you couldn't see yourself growing and you weren't getting any taller. Like my parents, my wife Heidi and I use our daughter Haiden's bedroom wall as a measuring tape to pencil in the date and record her current height. Even though Haiden doesn't feel she's growing, by looking back at the previous marks, she can see how much she has grown since the last recorded pencil mark.

Using records, graphs, measuring tools, or scales provides a baseline you can easily reference for motivation to keep chasing your goals. Looking back to lists of your written goals can be even more motivating. Measuring progress every step of the way is a great way to leverage change. And if you don't like the rate, pace, or length of your progression, then change it—you're in control!

WHAT DO YOU REALLY WANT?

I only ask this now, rather than at the end of this chapter in the *Think* section, because it's very important to know yourself to answer my next question.

Why don't you have what you want yet?

I believe it's because you haven't wanted it badly enough. You haven't truly decided what you want most, taken the steps to get there, or made it a priority. If you had done these things, I guarantee wanting it would no longer be necessary because you would already have it!

You'll always make time for what you prioritize as most important. If you don't already have what you want, maybe it isn't what you really desire. Desire is the driving force that catapults you to your goals and helps you obtain what you want most. However, if you are truly determined to reach your goals, you must maintain a strong desire that burns within you until you have that which you most want. English author and poet Rudyard Kipling said, "Not getting what you want either means you don't want it enough, or you have been dealing too long with the price you have to pay."

To get the things you truly want and reach the goals you most wish to reach, you'll have to break out of your comfort zone, breaking your own rules, and do things you've never done. Reaching your goal requires action, passion, and expanding your way of thinking. A different result will take changing the approach. You'll have to change the equation to your sum of 4!

HAVING A VISION

If you're unclear about yourself or what you want, you'll be unclear about your future and how to get what you want. Knowing exactly what you want is the first step in achieving your goals. The next step is creating a very vivid vision in your mind. Brazilian lyricist and novelist Paulo Coelho wrote, "Whenever you want to achieve something, keep your eyes open, concentrate, and make sure you know exactly what it is you want. No one can hit their target with their eyes closed."

A clear vision will increase your chance of success by helping define, measure, and focus your goals. A vision is essential because it acts as a target on which you as an individual, student, entrepreneur, or business leader can focus your energy and resources. A vision, much like a business, needs a plan that helps motivate and remind you of what and why you're doing the things you are doing. Unlike a dream, however, it's a reality—it just has not yet come to fruition!

Setting goals and creating a clear process of how to reach them only requires you to ask yourself what you want. Do you want to graduate from college, become a board member, be healthy, or have five million in the bank? Saying you want to be rich or famous isn't enough. You have to know precisely where you want to go or what you want. Once you know exactly what your destination is, what you want, or how you picture your life, it's much easier to get there.

Reed Sensei gave me the confidence, tools, and experience necessary to maintain focus on my goals and reach for the stars. He advised that if I wrote my goals down in great detail, I'd achieve or receive them. Whether it was attaining my black belt or living in Japan, if I'd write out my plan and place it somewhere I could see it every day as a reminder, reaching my goal was feasible and in my control. He often had words of wisdom, often similar in meaning, and always seemed to have the formula to crushing any limit or obstacle I faced. "You are capable of doing anything. Don't waste your time daydreaming and wishing you could. Visualize the best outcome, determine what you want, make it your number one priority, imagine the best way to get there, and then go get it!"

EASY AS ENTREPRENEURIAL PIE

In my life, I've never had a shortage of things I wanted to change, get better at, or become. For example, I wanted to reach the straddle splits, compete internationally in martial arts, go to business school, learn to speak multiple languages, live abroad, be the top-performing personal trainer, and become an international super model, actor, keynote speaker, and bestselling author.

With the exception of the bestselling author—time will tell—these goals have all been reached and crushed. Envisioning big goals and reaching for the stars has been easy for me, but prioritizing them was always my kryptonite or sticking point. During college, a true friend and schoolmate and I frequently teamed up and competed in entrepreneurial and business competitions. We both loved pitching new ideas in hopes of winning scholarships or start-up money and networking for internships or jobs.

Our senior year, we placed third in the business plan competition I thought we should have taken first in. Wanting to improve, I asked him what he thought I could have done better. He gave me great feedback that I believe helped us win the next competition and has stuck in my mind from that day forward:

> Blue, imagine that all your ideas represent a giant baked pie that's overflowing on your plate. You tend to take a bite here and there, from each individual piece, but never actually finish a whole piece, let alone the entire pie. Instead, I suggest choosing only two or three pieces, the ones that matter the most, set a realistic timeline for finishing each piece, stick to it, focus, and devote the majority of your time to just those pieces. That way, they each get anywhere from 33 to 50 percent of your time and have a greater chance of getting done. And if they aren't done within the timeframe you set, then it's either time to reevaluate the importance of the piece, readjust the timeline, or move on to a piece that is more of a priority.

Although I hate pie, his message was spot on. Priorities, like life, can change; what's important to us now may not be what it was in the past. I was not committing to any single course of action. I had too many ideas on my plate during the competition, and the most important ones weren't getting the attention needed to effectively complete them. To successfully reach my vision of who I wanted to be or what I wanted to accomplish would require four things: 1) I had to focus and prioritize the pieces, determining their value and purpose, 2) I had to set measurable, quantifiable, and realistic timelines for reaching each goal, 3) I had to stick to that timeframe, and if I didn't meet my specific timeline, I needed to adjust it or reevaluate the specific goal's importance, even if I still believed the vision was great. If it wasn't important enough, then putting it on the backburner or forgetting about it might be best, and 4) after reaching a goal or adjusting my priorities, I had to spend my time and energy on a new piece of pie.

ROAD TO THE STRADDLE SPLITS

Once you know what your goals are and have prioritized them, it's time to develop the strategic plan for getting there. Start with where you are now, then where you want to go, and then create a highlighted map with checkpoints for easily monitoring your progress.

Having watched too many Jean-Claude Van Damme movies, I wanted to copy his legendary splits. This is an example of a goal I had but had no clue how to attain. Other than seeing his progression in the movies, I had no realistic idea of the time, cost, pain, or path associated with achieving them. This highlights the importance of mapping out an efficient route from point A to where you want to be. I knew I wanted to get from A to Z, but just knowing I wanted to arrive at Z wasn't going to be enough.

Just imagine for a moment if you wanted to get from Seattle to Los Angeles by car. Before Google maps, smartphones, and even MapQuest, you didn't just get in a car and start driving in hopes of arriving in LA in a reasonable timeframe. Instead, you needed a predetermined plan or glove compartment map to find the quickest route, where to stay overnight, how many quick stops would be needed, and which roads to take. Ensuring we navigate our life's goals successfully requires the same methodical planning as driving cross-country. To do the straddle splits and use that flexibility in martial arts, I needed the quickest, safest, and most effective route possible.

First and foremost, I alone was in control to prioritize my vision. Therefore, I made becoming flexible a priority. Next, I asked others who had the flexibility I wanted to share what steps they took to get there. Third, I investigated via books, thanks in part to Reed Sensei's mini-library, on stretching, kinesiology, and how the body and muscles work. Fourth, I pooled all the research and advice I'd gathered and then set specific benchmarks and a timeline to track my progression toward reaching the straddle or center splits.

One must get to A before B, and B before reaching C, and so on. Disclaimer: If reaching the splits happens to be one of your goals, avoid rushing from A to C while avoiding B altogether. Skipping steps, when reaching for any goal, can hurt something fierce and tends not to be worth it in the long run. The final step in the entire process was to attain what I wanted. Therefore, I had to take action and just go for it. Consistency was somewhat difficult to maintain because of the residual pain associated from the previous days' stretching. However, rather than thinking that tomorrow would suffice, my motto became right now is even better. If the clock hasn't hit midnight yet, there's still time today.

By determining a roadmap for achieving the center splits, I could stay focused and consistent, see my progress, hold myself accountable, and easily adjust my routine if I wasn't seeing the results I wanted to see. Following this roadmap was the overwhelming factor in eventually being able to do the pancake or straddle splits. Long-lasting change and positive transformation aren't one or two seconds away; the choices you make in this moment will help push and project you toward your destination.

MENTOR/MENTEE

Randy Johnson was already a good pitcher in the major leagues when he had a face-to-face talk with the all-time great Nolan Ryan about the possibility of changing his delivery to improve his consistency. Accepting his need to change something, Johnson took Ryan up on his offer to spend some time working on his technique. They adjusted his mechanics and, even at 6' 10", how to be more aggressive, and it worked wonders. By making slight changes and not being afraid to do so, he got better and better. After winning 259 games, five Cy Young Awards, and being inducted into the Baseball Hall of Fame in 2015, Johnson credits Ryan for making him a better player on and off the field, saying, "Nolan also helped me learn how to be a better teammate and mentor. I'm enjoying baseball more than ever because I'm in a position to pass it on and help some of the younger players, like Nolan helped me."

SUMMARY

Life without change can be scarier than the act of changing itself. Seeking and committing to change is no easy task, but by accepting and embracing it, you are free to succeed and grow. Those with vision possess an internal compass, a control and navigational system for successfully reaching their targets. They create their own roadmap and make course changes or corrections only when they'll be productive or more efficient. Creating a vision, setting goals with realistic timelines, prioritizing what's most important to you, and then planning the most efficient route to your destination will guarantee getting what you want and creating a better you.

ACTION STEPS

THINK

Where would you like to see yourself now, in five years, and in ten years? List one for each timeline.

Now: _____

Five Years: _____

Ten Years: _____

Being true to yourself and your beliefs, brainstorm for five minutes about the things you'd like to change about your life and things you'd like to do or goals you would like to attain. Do this before moving on to the next step. Don't put limits on your ideas, goals, or dreams. Focus on what's most important to you, like a bucket list of your greatest ideas. Set the timer!

After your five-minute brainstorming session, write down the three you believe or imagined are the most important things you'd like to change about your life. Think of the pie example; take the three pieces that matter most to you and prioritize them in ascending order.

1. _____
2. _____
3. _____

Now take your three pieces of pie and create a list with timelines for each of them. Set measurable, definite, and quantifiable goals for reaching them. Do this by making to do lists of what's necessary for moving you closer to your goal. Remember to set realistic timelines when determining your roadmap to ensure you are seeing positive momentum for each one before crossing it off your list.

Change 1: _____

_____

_____

_____

Change 2: _____

_____

_____

_____

Change 3: _____

_____

_____

_____

DO

Clarify your vision or goal, and don't let it be unrealized. Get it out of your head and onto paper.

Remember to stay focused and keep your goals visible at all times. Keep them on your desk, in your car, on the refrigerator, in your wallet or purse, or on your bathroom mirror—anywhere you can see them every day. This will plant the seeds of success in your mind and help remind you of this piece of pie's importance. Your priorities may change, but keep the momentum moving in the direction you want.

Have a clear picture of where you're going and how you'll get there. Be specific and laser-focused on one direction.

Goal setting is putting your energy into something you can control. Commit to a single course of action and follow your roadmap until you achieve your goal. Then move on to the next goal.

Last, but not least, start! Take immediate action. Do this now, not tomorrow or next week. Begin right now before moving on to the next chapter. It's time to plant your tree!

4

MENTOR · DEVELOP · EXECUTE · **SUCCEED**

CHAPTER 18

TURNING YOUR PASSION INTO SUCCESS

"Find something that makes you happy and go for it."

— Zendaya

In the last chapter, we focused on the reasons behind and the benefits of seeking, accepting, and embracing change in all aspects of life. Being open to transformation allows us to positively and exponentially grow mentally and physically. We also discussed the importance of knowing who we really are and what we really want. Once we are comfortable with these truths, we can definitively create a roadmap to success. This measurable and realistic guide will help us become our best selves.

In this chapter, we'll use what you discovered in the last chapter to help identify what you're most passionate about, and then we'll look at how to turn that passion into an unstoppable force that steadily accelerates your success.

What moves you or sparks a fire under you enough that you would work all day for free? Is it something you love doing or that you can talk about naturally without ever tiring of it? Can you remember a time when you wanted something so badly that it was all you could think about day and night? Something that you'd put all your time, money, and energy into. We now want to find the answers to these questions to expose what you are most passionate about.

A MULLIGAN

Many of us have taken a personality test or career assessment at some point. Maybe it was the Myers-Briggs type indicator, Keirsey Temperament Sorter, MAPP, or some other self-assessment test. By answering the questions honestly, the results provide insight into who you are and what you should be doing with your life.

Okay, maybe none of these tests can precisely do that, but they do help identify your interests, strengths, weaknesses, and skills. This information can help you pick a major or identify a career you might get job satisfaction and fulfillment from. As actress and comedian Lucille Ball once said, "It's a helluva start, being able to recognize what makes you happy."

Since there are no correct answers, the tests aren't perfect and the results can be skewed by biased or dishonest answers. There may be gaps between the test measurements of what your true talents are, and what you really would enjoy doing for the rest of your life. But they can help with self-discovery, identifying ways to work from your talents, and give a better understanding of your motivations.

In high school, I suffered from confirmation bias and read the test results like a horoscope, believing only what I wanted. If I didn't like the results, like a mulligan in golf, I'd take the test a second time. Only this time, I would answer differently in hopes of manipulating the results so they would direct me toward something I believed I wanted, which was corporate business. However, no matter how I answered or tried to skew the test in favor of wearing a three-piece suit, the results were always the same. Much to my dismay, they consistently directed me toward becoming a teacher and entrepreneur.

The last thing I wanted to be was a teacher standing in front of a classroom scribbling on a giant chalkboard. Teaching didn't interest me, especially since I'd seen movies like *Stand and Deliver, The Principal, Wild Cats,* and *Dangerous Minds* where the classroom was no picnic.

And an entrepreneur? I couldn't even spell it, let alone understand what it meant.

Life and karma can sometimes be quite funny. It's been more than twenty-five years since I took my first career personality assessment, and it predicted the exact path my career took. After starting several successful businesses, consulting, teaching, instructing, and coaching every single day, the results were apparent. The tests had told the truth; I just hadn't yet realized a teacher doesn't just teach in a school and can come in many different forms—and I certainly learned how to spell the word entrepreneur.

FINDING YOUR PASSION

There's tremendous power in finding what drives you forward through the ups and downs, what fuels your burning desire, gives you purpose, and brings you real happiness. Experiencing the intense power and energy created by focusing on what most excites you is what passion is all about. Following your passion allows you to attain whatever you most want and stay focused until you have it. People who have found their passion are hungry, persistent, obsessed, and determined to achieve their objectives. French philosopher Denis Diderot once wrote, "Only passions, great passions, can elevate the soul to great things."

If you want to gain the upper hand, find happiness, achieve success, and reach the pinnacle of your career, you must understand what sets you on fire by discovering your passion. When you find and pursue your passion, everything else falls into place. A leader, mentor, coach, friend, or anyone else who follows their passion, signals to others that they are genuine and have real ambitions, expertise, experience, and direction. Others are attracted to and will follow and support them because they're excited to go to work every day and love what they're doing.

Your ideal career is something you love and enjoy doing every day. Everyone has something that makes them feel alive, passionate, or driven. Something you're excited to do every day is worth chasing and gives you fulfillment and purpose. It is a career where you can say, "I have the best job ever."

Discovering what excites and energizes you is the next step. Primetime Emmy Award winner and comedian Wanda Sykes said, "If you feel like there's something out there that you're supposed to be doing, if you have a passion for it, then stop wishing and just do it."

Stop procrastinating, being complacent, and accepting mediocrity. If you're unhappy, bored, unenthusiastic, or plain tired of your current situation, get out there and find what truly energizes and ignites a raging fire within you.

This discovery doesn't have to be difficult. It can come in many different forms. Although assessments and tests can be helpful, they aren't always the most reliable or accurate indicators when it comes to finding what you're most passionate about. Sometimes, simply asking others close to you for advice or reaching out to a mentor or coach can help you discover your passion.

After college and experiencing a sixth knee surgery, I briefly entertained the thought of becoming an anesthesiologist. Before every surgery, the coolest and funniest person in the operating room was the anesthesiologist. They would make me, the patient, feel comfortable and relaxed, literally and figuratively. They would tell me jokes and tell me to count down from a hundred as the anesthesia took effect. And, according to my own medical billing statements, it was a highly paid profession.

Entertaining the idea, I asked a close friend's dad who was an anesthesiologist to lunch to discuss the ins and outs of his career choice. He agreed to meet, to get an inside perspective. which turned out to be greatly beneficial. Knowing him personally was the icing on the cake. I'm forever grateful because he was candid and tailored his answers specifically to me. He said:

> I love my job because it's a great fit for me. The pay is good. I get to help others, and I get to play the part of a magician when I concoct cool recipes to put people to sleep. With this said, becoming an anesthesiologist isn't easy. It takes more schooling than just becoming a doctor—four years of med school and three to seven more as an intern or resident. Then another year of taking board tests. This is a great way to go into debt and stressful enough to make your hair turn gray early. (He pointed to his graying hair.) There's no room for error when putting someone under. Therefore, our profession pays the highest liability insurance rates. Also, because I know you're an extrovert and extremely active, I think you'd be bored by the work envi-

ronment. My work schedule and hours are all over the place, and it's hard to commit to anything outside of work or with the family. Also, once the patient goes night-night, I sit silently while focusing on a screen for hours. Blue, you tend to only see the best parts of my job. You need to look at the whole thing.

In twenty minutes, I was informed, guided, and warned by a professional with firsthand experience to think twice before starting a career in something that probably wouldn't bring me joy, fulfillment, or purpose. Simply by asking a first-hand source for insight—and it helped that he knew me—I realized pursuing this career presented more cons for me than pros and would most likely be a mistake for me. Based on his feedback, I knew I'd never truly enjoy or feel fulfilled as an anesthesiologist. As American author and screenwriter Ray Bradbury once said, "If you don't love something, then don't do it."

SIMPLY BRAINSTORM

The least expensive and possibly most effective path to finding your passion is simply to spend a moment and transcribe your thoughts on paper or online with a free brainstorming site. Brainstorming is designed to help spark, create, and organize your ideas visually. In finding your passion, the ideas must be things that excite you, things you truly value or love, and things you want to do or accomplish. A few examples might be money, travel, a job title, health, fame, living on a beach, or being a top sales rep.

Now, take just a moment and mentally try to create a career, your career, with as many of your loves as you can. Once you have one that contains most of your loves, you'll have found a career that can make you happy, give you great satisfaction, and you can be passionate about. As American steel magnate Charles M. Schwab once wrote, "A person can succeed at almost anything for which they have unlimited enthusiasm."

I've continuously updated, added to, or reevaluated my brainstorm sheet over the years. I've always loved helping others, martial arts, languages, reading and learning, money, travel, time with friends, being my own boss, movies, and health and fitness. Everything I loved, was enthusiastic about, and wanted bad enough to prioritize and not give up on, was right in front of me.

Therefore, I placed my sheet where I could see it every day as a reminder not to quit or give up. I found or made a way to make it happen. I then put all my energy toward achieving anything I wrote on that piece of paper because I only wrote down things I truly loved and wanted. I believed in myself and my ability, so I followed Nike's famous slogan and just did it!

THE BOWFLEX GUY

As humans, we gravitate toward what we most love and believe to be true. To reiterate from the last chapter, once you know what your vision or goals are, and have prioritized them, it's time to develop the strategic plan/roadmap for getting there—a map that shows where you are now, where you want to go, and has clear checkpoints to monitor and evaluate your progress. A combination of using this highlighted plan, accompanied with your natural desires, will ignite your passion and trigger an emotional response to motivate you.

When I was in my early teens, I often saw advertisements featuring popular movie stars and professional athletes to appeal to buyers wanting to imitate them. From magazine covers, underwear boxes, billboards, music videos, commercials, and infomercials, the secret to having washboard abs, being attractive to someone, and gaining the physique of a Greek god was simply to buy what they were selling.

One evening, while watching an *A-Team* episode, I naively became entranced with the promise of quickly transforming my body to peak athletic performance, thanks in part to a home gym workout commercial for the original Bowflex machine. It starred a muscular actor with a perfectly defined and chiseled eight pack performing simple upper body workouts on the machine.

The advertisement had done its job by successfully reaching a thirteen-year-old boy who wanted the same body as the guy on screen. To get it, all I had to do was dial their toll-free number to receive a free, complimentary, no risk, no promise to buy, VHS video with information packet. A week later, after making that call on our rotary telephone, the demo tape arrived. My mom, a more seasoned consumer, questioned my interest in the machine when the info packet arrived. I told her, "If we had a Bowflex machine, it would make me look like the guy on screen."

With a slight laugh, she replied, "I promise that buying or using that machine will not make you look like him. He is getting paid for the job because he already looks like that."

After the motherly commercial interruption, I knew a few things for certain. One, at that price, I surely wasn't going to get one of these things for Christmas. Two, getting paid to look like that would be awesome! Three, I wanted to know how to become the next Bowflex guy.

Seeing as I wasn't getting this machine delivered to our home anytime soon, and being serious about wanting to look a certain way, I took it upon myself to find several gyms to work out at. Not knowing what I was doing, and before personal training became a multibillion-dollar industry, I asked people who were in great shape and already looked the way I wanted to look for help. Over the next several years, I learned about ways to build muscle, the importance of a healthy diet, nutrition, athletic performance, and kinesiology. Weightlifting, working out, and martial arts training became my focus.

This passion eventually morphed into a career as a personal trainer, strength coach, and self-defense instructor at Gold's Gym. Ironically, this is also where I was scouted by a talent scout for a local modeling and acting agency.

A PHONE CALL

Who knew, I just happened to fit a male model's basic size requirement of 6'1," 32 x 32 pant, 40 regular suit, medium shirt, and size 11 shoe. Soon after, I signed with my current Seattle modeling agency, took acting classes, researched and followed men's fashion, spent countless hours practicing and posing in front of mirrors, invested in headshots and a professional portfolio, surrounded myself with those who had more experience to learn from, went to numerous castings, and finally began booking campaigns, commercials, and photo shoots.

The dream of becoming an actor and model eventually became more than a pipe dream; it turned into a twenty-year-and-counting, successful, international career. A career that has taken me around the world, created long-lasting friendships, kept me in top shape, taught me numerous lessons, given me countless entertaining stories, and still allows me to tell people, "I love my job. It's the best job ever!"

It's not only great to get paid for doing what I love, but rewarding to see a career blossom and reach every goal I set—whether it was to have washboard abs, be on the cover of multiple magazines, be featured on an underwear box, act in a Hollywood movie, land a national or international commercial, work and collaborate with some of the industry's most famous and talented people, or travel the world. If you're passionate, your mind will follow your beliefs, goals, and expectations.

What would you choose to do if you were guaranteed success? Whatever the answer, quitting isn't an option because achieving your goal may be just around the next corner. Great success is always rooted in your greatest expectations and passions. Being passionate will make the journey to achieving these goals fulfilling and priceless. And let's not forget about the rewarding feeling you'll experience when you're able to cross goals or objectives off your list and replace them with new ones!

When I received a direct booking in Portland, Oregon, for a fitness company named Nautilus Inc., I had no idea what would soon come to fruition. Shortly after arriving on location, I checked in with the photoshoot's producer to get a rundown of the day's photo and video shot list and storyboard. She brought me back to the set to meet the photographer, the client, and the rest of the crew. There in the middle of the set, directly under the photo lights and in front of the camera, was the newest Bowflex machine. The producer told me Bowflex had recently been acquired by Nautilus, and I had a few minutes to relax and help myself to any snacks or beverages before meeting with the stylist and makeup artist. I was about to cross something off my list!

Instead of helping myself to the snack bar, I stepped outside and made an early morning phone call to my mom. When she answered, I said, "Guess who the new Bowflex guy is?"

Following my passion has not only opened doors and introduced me to a career I love, but it has simultaneously allowed me to generate other streams of income by doing jobs I truly enjoy. I feel fortunate that my career path has given me options and the ability to make informed decisions on other goals. Whether it's speaking, consulting, or instructing, my passions have not only fulfilled me, but more importantly, they have allowed me to financially defend, protect, and prepare myself for the unknown.

MENTOR/MENTEE

It was head coach Bill Belichick's decision to keep Tom Brady on the New England Patriots roster and not trade him away, even though he wasn't the best quarterback at the time. Belichick stuck with Brady, and as a result, they won six Super Bowls together. They are both deeply passionate about the game of football and about winning. They depend on their love for the game and their communication for success. As Belichick once said, "There are things he sees that I just don't see, and I think the reverse is true," and "I love football. I love learning about football. I think Tom is the same. I think we've learned from each other, and we've been able to grow together...."

SUMMARY

It's important to be aware of your capabilities, strengths, and weaknesses. Knowing who you are and what you love will help you find a life that is fun, fulfilling, and purposeful. No matter what your personality type is, being armed with the knowledge of which type best identifies you and your passions is the secret to achieving peak performance. Following your passion doesn't mean you have to settle for just one thing. Having a burning desire to do something and being passionate about what you do will help you storm fearlessly through life, give you multiple options and income streams, and bring out your best.

ACTION STEPS

THINK

List the ten things you love that bring you the most enjoyment. You can make a bigger list, but try to keep it to your top ten. You could list money, travel, fame, sports, the outdoors, swimming, food, baking, sunsets, yoga, etc. Be honest and remember there are no wrong answers—just list what you really think brings you the most happiness.

1. _____
2. _____
3. _____
4. _____
5. _____
6. _____
7. _____
8. _____

TURNING YOUR PASSION INTO SUCCESS

9. _____

10. _____

Now, take the ten items and list all the jobs you can create that include all or most of the ten things. Some career ideas might only include two or three combinations, others more than half, and maybe just one or two will include all ten. For example, using the ten examples above, here is a possible career breakdown:

A famous cook who travels the world and lives on the waterfront, visiting various health and wellness retreats as their guest chef.

See how many careers you can create with your top ten.

1. _____
2. _____
3. _____
4. _____
5. _____
6. _____
7. _____
8. _____
9. _____
10. _____

DO

Reach out to your support system and any tools available to help find your passion.

Follow your passion. Life is a path, and you can dictate where it takes you and how long it takes to get there.

Let whatever gives you a burning desire deep inside drive you toward the lifestyle, career, and relationships you want. Never stop following your passions or reaching for the stars. Turn them into a reality, and even multiple streams of income, by creating a laser-focused roadmap that clearly gets you to your ultimate destination.

4

MENTOR • DEVELOP • EXECUTE • **SUCCEED**

CHAPTER 19
BALANCING LIFE

"Never get so busy working that you forget to make a life."

— Dolly Parton

In the last chapter, we stressed the importance of turning your passion into success and creating a life and/or career from what you love most. It's possible as well as okay to love your job. By using the natural powers of your passion and surrounding yourself with those conducive to growth and momentum, you can fast-track your success in all aspects of life and enjoy the ride at the same time. Nothing can hold you back if you have a burning desire to accomplish your goals. Take your destiny into your own hands, and live a life driven by purpose.

This chapter's purpose is to understand that your goals, intentions, and enjoyment can be balanced and scheduled. This can be determined by what makes you happiest and gives you the most reward. We'll also look at seeking the perfect balance between your personal and career life to gain greater control over your life. There's only so much time in each day, so what's most important is how we allocate that time!

How much time each day do you spend mentally and physically at work? Does this make you feel your responsibilities are stretching you too thin and wish you had a better work-life balance?

WORK-LIFE BALANCE

A work-life balance, its value, and meaning differ for each of us. What's constant, however, is that it involves a mix of time management, commitment, and prioritizing. Finding the perfect mix can be stressful, whether it's trying to balance your hours at work, eating dinner at home with the family each night, spending time with friends, dropping kids off at school, or taking care of your own health.

Balancing and prioritizing these responsibilities and activities is difficult. And today, in our connected world, it is even harder to disconnect from our work duties, even when we're off the clock. Focusing on personal values by prioritizing and staying flexible with our limited time is the surest way to keep a work-life balance. Failing to find this balance can have lasting repercussions, as former COO and vice chairman of The Coca-Cola Company Brian Dyson said:

> Imagine life as a game in which you are juggling some five balls in the air… You will soon understand that work is a rubber ball. If you drop it, it will bounce back. But the other four balls—family, health, friends, and spirit—are made of glass. If you drop these, they will be irrevocably scuffed, marked, nicked, damaged, or even shattered. They will never be the same. You must understand that and strive for balance in your life.

Certain things require our undivided attention. Some things can be put aside, suspended, or postponed for a short period, but if they are neglected for too long, you run the risk of damaging them forever.

For example, a workaholic is someone who can't disconnect, who chooses to spend their entire day at work or working after hours. They forget to make time for themselves and those close to them. They forget or choose not to eat, stay active, spend time with their loved ones, relax, or decompress and take a vacation. In the short run, this constant, all-out sprint might work to move your career forward. In the long run, however, you'll burn out mentally and physically.

A car can run on either regular or premium gas. It doesn't have to have the oil changed every three-thousand miles, have the windshield wipers changed annually, or even be insured. It can even coast on an empty tank, but sooner or later, the lack of basic maintenance will kill it. Co-founder of *Medium* and *Twitter* Evan Williams said:

> Take care of yourself: When you don't sleep, eat crap, don't exercise, and are living off adrenaline for too long, your performance suffers. Your decisions suffer. Your company suffers. Love those close to you: the failure of your company is not failure in life. Failure in your relationship is.

INVEST IN YOUR HEALTH

Your body, mind, career, relationships, and family all require constant attention. If you forget to take care of yourself or you neglect the things important to you, someone or something will suffer or break. If you burn your candle at both ends for too long, you will make mistakes. Like a car, a person who maintains a great work-life balance not only has the energy to perform at peak levels, but also has the endurance, resilience, reliability, and durability to withstand life's potholes and stand the tests of time.

I mentioned earlier that I've had six knee surgeries due to a martial arts injury I've had to work through and overcome. The song "Dem Bones" is used to teach kids skeletal vocabulary and their locations as in: "The knee bone connected to the thigh bone/The thigh bone connected to the hip bone...."

This song also emphasizes how the body's kinetic chain works. Basically, the ends of your bones are connected by joints or segments that influence the joining bone's movement. Everything is connected, and when there's motion, it creates a chain of events that affect the movement of neighboring joints and segments. If there's a kink, knot, or broken link, the entire chain and its movements can suffer.

If I failed to rehab my knee correctly, I ran the risk that my hip or ankle could begin to take more of the workload, thus resulting in an ankle or hip injury. Much like a water balloon being stepped on, if you press down on it slowly, the water is displaced, shifts, and finds another place to be. Even worse, if you press too quickly or apply too much pressure on the balloon, the water won't have enough space or time to adjust or transfer its energy and the balloon will burst.

An overall healthy mental and physical lifestyle can help prevent injury, chronic disease, and long-term illness. Staying healthy and addressing any kink or broken pieces in your chain will help prevent future illness and injury. Diet and exercise help keep the body well fueled, maintained, and working properly. For your body to perform at peak levels, it needs a balanced diet, regular exercise, and enough sleep to recover and recharge. Taking care of ourselves mentally and physically may be the most important thing we can control. As celebrity personal trainer Jillian Michaels said:

Do you realize that there is nothing in our genes that tells us when to die? There are genetic codes that tell us how to grow, how to breathe, and how to sleep, but *nothing* that tells us to die. So why do we? Because we literally rust and decay our bodies from the inside out with poor food and lifestyle choices.

BATTERY LIFE

Having a healthy and balanced life requires making a conscious effort, personally and professionally, to maintain focus on health and balance. You must prioritize and find the right balance that works for you. It's so difficult to carve out time in our busy schedules to do everything we want to do. Along with the constant responsibilities, distractions and interruptions, we can feel so drained by the end of the day. This is especially true if one doesn't take the time to recharge their physical and mental energy.

Taking time to relax, refresh, and recharge is invaluable. Therefore, finding and knowing the best way for you is key. My wife Heidi, for example, plugs her phone or laptop in every night and throughout the day. I, on the other hand, wait until the battery is nearly or completely dead. Depending on who you ask, one method may be better for the device's battery. In the end, both methods get the job done, but we each use the method that makes us feel more comfortable.

Vacations are a similar example. Heidi loves to take lots of mini-vacations here and there throughout the year. Although I love taking vacations and would love to always be off work, I feel more relaxed and recharged when I take fewer vacations but for longer periods. Heidi and I just have different ways of reaching the same outcome. The equation that works best for me is $(2 + 2 = 4)$, while Heidi uses a different equation to feel fully recharged. No matter what formula we use, it's important to know what works best for each of us.

BALANCING ACT

Finding the right mix for an active, healthy, work-life balance is the ultimate goal. Being successful isn't about being great at one thing. You can't just be great at being present, attentive, in good physical shape, stress free, followed by millions on social media, getting raises, beating the competition, or solidifying sales. Success isn't always how much you have or what you've done, but how you've helped improve yourself and whom you've helped grow and improve.

Life isn't a buffet where you take what you like and leave the rest to rot. You're an entire package, and success depends on a healthy combination of everything on the buffet table. To find true balance, you must consider all the things that compete for your time, and then decide what to keep on your plate and what to leave for later. As referenced in Chapter 17, when choosing which slice of the pie to eat, select the most meaningful pieces, prioritize them, and then focus on them intently.

As a father and husband, I find it difficult to find a work-life balance that always works. The perfect mix for my family of three sometimes feels like a myth or fantasy because it is so hard to find. And when we get close, it changes. It constantly evolves. Especially when our jobs take us on the road or in the air. Family time can be quite elusive, and sometimes, I feel like the three of us get the short end of the stick.

My time in this world is limited, and I wish to spend that time with my friends and family. Even though I'm passionate about my career, I also know it won't be long before my daughter is all grown up. Therefore, I make sure there's enough time during or after work for my family. It's my role and responsibility to protect, provide, set aside, and powerfully guard the time required to be omnipresent and in the now. Walt Disney once said, "A man should never neglect his family for business."

You have to plan to have a successful work-life balance. Even fifteen minutes a day eating a meal together, doing a treasure hunt, playing catch, wrestling, playing with *Star Wars* toys (my favorite), or reading my daughter a story at bedtime is worth a thousand times more than fifteen minutes at work. Setting guidelines and priorities and making balance a habit will help illuminate what the perfect work-life combination means to you.

Do you know what your balance of work and personal life is?

While some lean toward career, family, or community, it's what you and your loved ones consider most important and well balanced that matters. Knowing what matters most to you, what makes you happy, allows you to strive to make time for it, whatever it is, and spend more time doing it.

MENTOR/MENTEE

Jillian Michaels credits Suze Orman for taking her under her wing, for her professional guidance and advice, and for teaching her how to balance her newfound fame. Michaels felt she was an expert in the fitness industry, but she knew she needed to learn to protect herself legally after becoming a high-profile star. Michaels didn't want to devote all her time to something she wasn't an expert at.

She talked to Orman, who helped her find balance between running a business, fame, and doing what you are passionate about.

SUMMARY

You must make deliberate choices about what you want from life, how you spend your day, and what success means to you. This mix must include time to reenergize your mental and physical wellbeing. Dedicating too much time to one thing, while neglecting or avoiding something else, can have disastrous consequences—burnout, bankruptcy, injury, death, banishment, divorce, or failure. These repercussions can be avoided by having a healthy work-life balance and setting guidelines on how you spend time.

ACTION STEPS

THINK

How do you balance your life currently? In what ways could you improve this balance?

_____

_____

How can you adjust your priorities to avoid neglecting any of your responsibilities or the things most important to you?

_____

_____

List three things you are responsible for that you would like to improve and be more proactive about. Include a realistic timeline for each item. Then commit to following that plan and regularly checking in or reevaluating this balance.

1. _____
2. _____
3. _____

DO

Begin lifting weights with someone; start running or walking with friends; cook together as a family; devote your undivided attention for at least fifteen minutes a day to your family or closest friends, take a one-week "stay-cation," monthly mini-vacation, or yearly two-week vacation. The bottom line is to find the best way to feel fully charged.

Invest in yourself! Don't neglect your health, education, experiences, career, relationships, or family. Avoid irreversible or costly consequences by devoting the time necessary to what you're most responsible for and what brings you the most happiness.

Make deliberate choices about what you want and how you spend your time. Spend your time doing what makes you happiest and predetermine how to allocate the time, effort, and energy to fulfill yourself.

4

MENTOR · DEVELOP · EXECUTE · **SUCCEED**

CHAPTER 20
BELIEVING IN YOURSELF

"If your actions inspire others to dream more, learn more, do more, and become more, you are a leader."

— John Quincy Adams

Finding the right recipe to balance your work and personal life was the focus of the last chapter. Discovering the proper mixture of things relevant and important to you and then devoting defined time and effort to it is the secret to a more joyful and fulfilling work-life balance.

Now that we've reached this book's final chapter, we'll come full circle to see how a scared and insecure young boy learned many of life's most important lessons and habits, including how to believe in himself and eventually become an inspirational leader and mentor, through a variety of vastly different components.

Through these different career paths and leadership roles, I've realized the benefits of becoming an inspiration to thousands of people. Therefore, uncovering your hidden talent and learning the benefits of unlocking your ability to inspire, influence, and mentor is the focus of this final chapter.

BELIEVE IN YOURSELF

Believing in yourself is a critical step in succeeding in everything you do or dream of doing. How you look at life can determine your mood and your outlook on everything. By thinking and talking positively to yourself, you instantly subvert your negative and discouraging thoughts throughout your day. High-achieving individuals subconsciously tend to use positive language or speak positively to themselves. Author Watty Piper perfectly highlighted the value of optimism, positive language, and hard work when he wrote, "I think I can. I think I can. I think I can. I know I can."

The way we talk to ourselves makes a big difference. Saying, "I have to work out tonight," is much different than saying, "I get to work out tonight." They both indicate you're working out tonight, but one has a positive tone, while the other is negative. The specific words used can change the meaning, resulting in a drastically different outcome. Your thoughts become your words, and your words become your actions. How we talk to ourselves gives us the power to create or destroy. We are defined by what we say and believe.

Believing in yourself is a superpower. The movie *Crazy, Stupid, Love* hits on this point perfectly. Let me set the mood of this rom-com in case you haven't seen it. Steve Carell plays a family man whose wife admits to having an affair, and he becomes a sad case, feeling sorry for himself.

Ryan Gosling plays an accomplished, very charming, well-dressed, and super-confident bachelor. Gosling takes pity on Carell and mentors him with an honest, tough love approach. He tells Carell the reason he's lost his wife isn't because of another man, but because he no longer believes in himself and has lost sight of who he is as "a man, a husband, and probably a lover." Zing!

One of my favorite scenes is when Gosling takes Carell on an expensive shopping spree. Carell starts the scene in terribly bland "dad" clothes that don't fit and have no style, symbolizing how he's let himself go and become invisible to everyone, including his family. With no style of his own, Carell looks submissive, weak, and dopey in his Gap jeans. In contrast, Gosling's character is the exact opposite—sharply dressed with a confident personality that takes him wherever he wants to go. Gosling's character knows the importance of believing in yourself, having a great style, and a strong personal appearance. Carell's Gap pants and New Balance shoes didn't make a strong impression and weren't helping him succeed. Therefore, Gosling reminds Carell by saying, "Be better than the Gap."

Remember my story about the instructor who knew he'd defeated me before class even started? Much of the self-doubt I'd experienced came from consistently telling myself I could never win against him. The opposite is also true because if you continue to tell yourself you believe in yourself, eventually, you'll really exude confidence. It's that simple! Take it from six-time NBA all-star, MVP, and three-time NBA Championship winner Stephen Curry, who said, "To excel at the highest level—or any level, really—you need to believe in yourself."

WHAT'S A TABATA?

High-Intensity Interval Training (HIIT) has become very popular in the fitness world. Unlike typical cardiovascular training, it's designed to get your heart rate up very quickly to an extreme anaerobic zone. Tabata training is a very challenging and specific type of HIIT training. It was designed and developed to support the Japanese speed-skating team by scientist Dr. Izumi Tabata to increase maximal oxygen uptake (VO2 max) and anaerobic (without oxygen) capacity during workouts.

These workouts involve eight rounds of twenty-second, all-out-effort training, followed by ten seconds of rest per round. The work-rest ratio was proven to be one of the best ways to burn more calories and improve overall athletic performance. These twenty-second bursts of sprint style may be short and seem easy at first glance, but they take everything you have to keep performing at your highest level.

The moment you get distracted, even for a few seconds, the workout becomes less effective. You have to believe you can do it, and talking positively to yourself inspires you to push yourself through the pain. Knowing deep down that you can do anything all-out for at least twenty seconds makes the exercise possible and keeps self-doubt in check.

On a side note, if you're looking for a great way to spice up your workouts and only have a short time, I challenge you to throw any Tabata combination into your exercise routine. Good luck, and remember the chant of The Little Engine That Could! Repeating positive phrases like "I think I can. I think I can" to yourself with power and conviction will bring endless physical and mental rewards.

Whether it's your first time trying to squat a certain weight, audition for a lead role in a movie, ask for a raise, give a public speech, run a 5K, or argue a case in front of the Supreme Court, if you don't believe in yourself and keep going, you can't expect anyone else to believe in you. If you're a corporate leader for example, you can't expect your employees to fully R.E.L.A.T.E. or believe in you, if you don't even believe in yourself.

If you allow self-doubt to seep into your subconscious, it can destroy your heart, mind, body, and soul. The power of belief can change the world. Truly believing in yourself gives you ultimate confidence, and in theory, makes you indestructible and immortal. Remember the only one who can tell you "no" is yourself. You're in the pilot's seat, so you might as well sit back, relax, and enjoy the flight.

THE CIRCLE IS COMPLETE

Life is never a straight line; it has many paths with interesting twists and turns that are unique to us, yet similar to those experienced by others. Sometimes, even while in the driver's seat, things can turn out to be quite ironic. For example, I tried to avoid being a teacher and entrepreneur, but in the end, that's exactly who and what I became. My life came full circle, starting as a young mentee and eventually becoming a leader and mentor myself.

Spending years surrounded by a support system that encouraged me to become the best I could be, by people with R.E.L.A.T.E., I naturally began to see the benefits of inspiring others as a leader myself. They all, one way or another, encouraged me to be a better leader and mentor. Almost by accident, as my experiences, skill sets, and expertise increased, so did my roles in leadership.

Reed Sensei, in particular, took great satisfaction at bringing out the best out in me. He not only taught me the lessons I have shared with you, but he was the key factor in my becoming a teacher, instructor, and leader. We both love and loved guiding and mentoring others because of the deep satisfaction we get from helping others reach their full potential.

He accomplished this at first, when I was in my early teens, by using me as a model to help explain and demonstrate proper technique in the class. Then, as a black belt, he began having me teach the younger students. Not only did teaching give me valuable teaching experience, but it provided me with insight into gaps in my own techniques. He believed to be an expert at something you first had to be able to effectively teach it and pass that knowledge onto someone else.

Inadvertently, I've applied this theory to every passion I've followed. Whether it was working with a scuba company in Mexico, being on a construction crew, as a self-defense instructor, personal trainer, strength coach, professional model, actor, keynote speaker, or as a parent, I started as a learner and became an expert by passing my experience and knowledge on. As Darth Vader, the Sith Lord himself, said to his former mentor Obi-Wan Kenobi, "We meet again, at last. The circle is now complete. When I met you, I was but the learner. Now, I am the master."

HELPING OTHERS SUCCEED

Helping people learn and grow their skills and knowledge is an amazing feeling. Making a difference in someone's life is not only one of the greatest rewards, but something we all have the opportunity and ability to do. As noted in Chapter 6, surrounding yourself with people you can depend on when it matters most is invaluable. Being the one who shows up and helps others is priceless as well!

As I created a team of mentors from all kinds of backgrounds throughout my life, I began to find pleasure and reward by reciprocating support and guidance. I found joy and happiness in assisting or mentoring someone else. It's fair to say I found a new passion in helping others succeed, one my assessment tests had discovered years before. The great artist and painter Pablo Picasso once wrote, "The meaning of life is to find your gift. The purpose of life is to give it away."

Much like the act of tithing in the biblical sense, mentoring is giving back, sacrificing your own time, and contributing your knowledge and energy to provide for those less fortunate, less informed, or just learning a new skill, with a cheerful heart. And like tithing, the overall act of giving is more powerful and emotionally rewarding than that which you give away. Just as boxing great Muhammad Ali once said, "Service to others is the rent you pay for your room here on earth."

Knowing you've directly helped others grow, develop, advance their careers, and improve their skills can enrich your life and be personally fulfilling. Seeing your mentee, student, employee, colleague, or child succeed as a result of your input is the ultimate reward. The personal satisfaction I gain knowing I can make a difference in someone's life, like Reed Sensei and so many others have done and still do for me today, is why I continue to strive to encourage, guide, and help others on their own journeys. What you pass along to others will come back to you like a boomerang.

PEOPLE ARE LIKE ONIONS

There's no finish line in life! I don't mean every time you draw a line in the sand, the line goes out farther and farther. I mean there's no perfect ending or happily ever after. You set a goal, achieve it, and then set a new one. Your life and career are one giant learning curve that takes constant learning, work, and effort not only to become successful, but to stay there. It is a race being held in a classroom that can be slow or fast, all alone or as a team. Now, let me call on you as a student and ask you a simple question:

What's your favorite color? (No bonus points for you if it happens to be my name, *Blue*!)

Now, for something more difficult: Do you know your child's, spouse's, parent's, partner's, best friend's, or boss' favorite color? Are you thankful you're not on live television, next to a buzzer, on an episode of *Family Feud*? Congratulations, if you don't have to ask them. If you don't know, read the next question before running to ask them.

Now for the really hard and more detailed portion of both the above questions.

Why is that your favorite color? And can you explain *why* those are their favorite colors?

If these questions stump you, don't be alarmed—that is normal. Knowing your own or someone else's favorite color is like seeing the outer layer of an onion. Knowing the *why* is an even deeper layer to that onion. Like onions, we humans have layers, and those layers define who we are, define our values, and can explain why we act, say, or do what we do. Most of us never look further than the surface or outer layer of someone else.

Knowing why your kid's favorite color is purple, for example, means knowing them that much deeper, and having a greater connection and understanding of how they tick. It could be that they loved

Happy Meals and the character Grimace from McDonald's. Or they loved singing, "I love you, you love me...," or some other sappy Barney song. (Sorry Barney lovers.) Maybe it could be that they love the smell of lilacs, or it reminds them of picking fresh plums with the family during a memorable vacation.

The point is a great deal of effort is needed to truly know someone. This deep understanding exemplifies how involved you choose to be in those you work with, teach, lead, mentor, converse with, live with, or are related to. It's not an easy process and takes sacrifice to communicate with others in a positive way!

This is the way to peel onions, and it's the way to become a strong and influential person. It is about having the ear and trust of those around you. To peel back someone's layers, you must put others before yourself, share advice, and invite others to share their own insights. This two-way street is the way to build your leadership skills, improve your ability to communicate, advance your career, and formulate your heart by helping others persevere.

Class is in session, and you get to be the student or the professor. Your life is full of many lessons you've learned along the way. Some lessons were hard, some were easy. You don't have to be a leader, teacher, coach, or instructor to make a difference in someone's life. The mere act of helping someone better themselves and sharing your wisdom and experiences is one of the greatest gifts you can give. Author and life coach Lynda Field once said, "If you want to attract positive things into your life, then begin now by spreading positive energy about."

Are you ready to help someone, even if it's just for a moment, to succeed or improve in some way? Your advice may not always be taken, but it should always be available. Being a strong, inspirational leader doesn't require a specific title. Instead, I've suggested throughout this entire book that it only takes believing you can offer yourself as a mentor. You have all the tools and skills necessary to help and encourage others to persevere and prosper. Believe in yourself, and stay positive. Know that you can make a difference. Now, I challenge you to see what you can offer, how you can guide, assist, teach, or mentor someone.

MENTOR/MENTEE

Astronaut and former US Senator John Glenn credits his high school civics teacher for making his youth very rewarding by stressing the importance of believing in yourself and the significance of giving back. Glenn once said about his teacher, "He is an advocate of mentoring and has spoken about the importance of being a mentor. I think a mentor gets a lot of satisfaction in a couple of ways. They're doing something constructive, so they feel good about that. And when they see the results of this, with the young people they're working with, it's very, very rewarding."

SUMMARY

Your chance of succeeding is greatly enhanced by believing in yourself. Every goal you set will depend on this belief. People will follow you when you have confidence in yourself. It's that simple! Believing in yourself is one of the most powerful choices you have, so don't waste any time or effort on self-doubt.

See past the surface of people who come into your life and make an effort to pull back their outer layers to create a two-way street with a greater understanding of them. You can enrich your life on a personal and professional level by helping and giving away your time and energy. The benefits are overwhelming when you provide guidance that motivates and inspires others to fulfill their potential. Not to mention the deep personal satisfaction of sharing skills and experiences with a willing and grateful learner.

ACTION STEPS

THINK

How do you motivate yourself through challenges? Are you a glass half empty or half full personality?

_____

_____

Is there someone you believe could truly benefit from your experience and knowledge? Write down three names of people you could guide or mentor starting this week. Add how you will help them.

1. _____
2. _____
3. _____

DO

Dedicate time each day to self-belief. Deflect the doubt, stress, and fear that can creep in when stretching to accomplish any goal or task beyond your comfort zone. Drown out negativity.

Reread this book, the mini-stories, chapter titles, or the inspirational quotes as often as you need to stay positive, motivated, and inspired. Persevere and bring out your natural best. Stay focused and engaged with yourself and, most importantly, believe in yourself.

Give yourself pep-talks and repeat positive phrases.

I challenge you to ask one person a week for six months (a total of at least twenty-six people) if they could use a word of advice, help, assistance, or just someone to bounce an idea off.

Create a better understanding of two-way communication. Get to know the people you engage daily on a deeper level. Attempt to peel back a layer of their onion.

Think of yourself as a life coach to those who can benefit from your guidance, skills, and experience. Listen first, give honest feedback, have mutual respect, engage in two-way communication, be available, motivate, and inspire. Find the way they get to "4."

Pay it forward!

4

MENTOR • DEVELOP • EXECUTE • **SUCCEED**

A FINAL NOTE

"If you cannot see where you are going, ask someone who has been there before."

— J. Loren Norris

Now we come to the end of this book, but the start of your new journey. Armed with what we've discussed cover to cover, I once again ask you a set of difficult questions. Now that you've finished this self-help book, what are you going to do about it? How will you apply the sum of 4 to any obstacle, dream, or goal? What mentors will you intentionally seek out, or how will you react to those you unintentionally meet? What will you do to foster and stimulate those relationships? Who can you mentor, and what relationships can you embrace?

This is your pivotal call to action (CTA) moment to take a chance and embrace change. I want you to use this book as the resource it was intended to be, as a virtual mentor, to improve your personal and professional life. I challenge you to apply everything and every story I've shared. Without application, the lessons will merely be entertaining stories. A lack of action will leave you no better off than you were before turning the first few pages. The book's message will not work unless you apply it. This is where the journey begins, so it is time to plant that tree.

Time to shake off the cobwebs and use the ten blank lines below to write down ten actions you can commit to taking over the next ninety days. Maybe you want to buy a house, pay off your car, enroll in a skill-specific class, lose fifteen pounds, write your own book, reread this book, give a motivational speech, take your employees to lunch, get married, or join a mentoring club. Whatever you're doing in the next ninety days, I want you to know you've been inspired as a result of reading this book. I want you to be the person who musters the courage to step beyond your comfort zone and commit fully by writing out these ten actions right now.

1. _____
2. _____
3. _____
4. _____
5. _____
6. _____
7. _____
8. _____
9. _____
10. _____

When you were a child, your parents were superheroes. As an adult, strong leaders and mentors can be your superheroes. By reading this book, you learned firsthand the importance of finding and surrounding yourself with mentors who can push you beyond your limits and crush your own self-limiting limits. Those whom you Respect, wish to Emulate, Love, Admire, Trust, and Empathize with. This is the secret ingredient that serves as the catalyst for maximizing personal growth and improvement and shedding years off any learning curve.

You've learned the true power of mentoring, and how to develop a plan to harness its power. Plus, you've learned to set realistic goals with tangible timelines and how to create a roadmap to get where you want and are meant to be. Your destination!

Perhaps the biggest lesson to remember is that there is more than one way to get to any desired result. Water can move past a rock by going to the left, right, over, under, or even through it. Knowing there are multiple, if not infinite, ways to solve life's challenges, and finding the most effective path is the driving force behind the methodology of *The Sum of 4*. The fight is never over. Just as the opportunity to grow and learn hasn't passed. When you fall, the real fight is just beginning, and that is the point at which you must fight harder than ever. If your life is at stake, you don't just give up; you fight back sometimes by any means necessary, thinking outside the box, or finding alternate paths.

The reason you're not where you want to be yet is because the roadmap and traction needed to get to your goals wasn't obvious until now. It's now time to roll up your sleeves and challenge yourself to achieve your full potential and share it with others. If you apply the wisdom of this book, you will not only fast-track your self-leadership skills, but accelerate your success in all aspects of life. If you do, I promise you'll achieve heights you never imagined, crush any limits you or someone else sets, live a fulfilled life, and be surrounded by those who R.E.L.A.T.E. to you. If you can do these things, you'll have learned the true power of mentorship, becoming a better leader, and becoming someone others want to follow.

Now that you've finished this book, please let me know what it did for you. What did you learn? How did it speak to you? I'd also like to know what your life is like at this moment. What challenges and obstacles do you face? Please tell me how I can help you. Share your story. Perhaps we can talk by phone, or better yet, book me to travel to your location to speak to you or your organization.

I would like to offer you an initial, no-obligation, complimentary mentoring and coaching consultation. Please feel free to contact me. My email is blue@bluestiley.com. Be sure to include your name, time zone, and contact information so we can coordinate your complimentary consultations via phone, FaceTime, or in person. Let me become your mentor and see how I can help you achieve your goals.

I thank you for trusting me and finishing this book. I hope you were encouraged by the stories and examples. I hope you apply these lessons and exercises with anyone and everyone you come across. Let this be the beginning for us, not the end.

I wish you all the success, prosperity, fulfillment, love, and happiness this world has to offer. I believe in you and wish you the courage, confidence, and strength to reach your goals and fulfill your passions. I know you have the power to control your own destiny.

Often, the small choices we make greatly influence the trajectories of our lives. This is one of those pivotal moments when you have the power to act. You can lead an extraordinary life. Everything you want in business and life is within your reach, so seize your moment. Stop waiting, stop making excuses, close the gap, start doing, and start living.

Make a difference, be strong, and become legendary!

Your friend,

Blue Stiley

At age eight, the day I met Technical Sergeant Robey R. Reed.
1984

ABOUT THE AUTHOR

BLUE STILEY is an author, professional keynote speaker, life and business strategist, self-leadership and empowerment coach, health and wellness coach, and entrepreneur. He first discovered his gift for mentoring, coaching, and speaking to various audiences at the age of thirteen while teaching youth martial arts classes. Since then, and with more than thirty years of self-leadership, empowerment, and coaching experience, Blue has inspired, mentored, and motivated audiences and individuals nationally and internationally to become the best they can be.

Blue has developed and implemented programs for thousands of students, Olympic athletes, celebrities, fashion models, CEOs, entrepreneurs, business leaders, executives, small business owners, and everyday people through presentations, classes, seminars, workshops, and one-on-one coaching and private sessions. Blue founded Shadow Fitness (ShadowFitness.com) in 2006, a private training studio and online website that has brought some of the best and brightest health and wellness professionals in the industry together from around the world.

He has traveled the world, lived in more than three countries, and speaks multiple languages. Blue got his first business license at the age of twelve so he could sell sports cards. This early entrepreneurial endeavor eventually paid for his entire college education. He's a martial arts expert, personal trainer, strength coach, and has competed as an elite athlete worldwide. Blue was awarded 2003

Top Trainer North Seattle Gold's Gym and 2003 Trainer of the Year. He has received certifications in everything from personal training to holding multiple black belt ranks in various martial arts.

Blue is represented internationally and nationally as an actor and fashion model. He has worked in film for nearly twenty years with clients such as Volvo, Disney, Amazon.com, Nike, REI, Nordstrom, Coors, Eddie Bauer, Microsoft, The Seattle Seahawks, Starbucks, Hanna Andersson, Jockey, Nautilus, Turkish Airlines, Adidas, Tommy Bahama, Subaru, Walmart, Levi's, and Men's Wearhouse, to name just a few.

Originally from Washington, Blue attended college in Japan and graduated from the Foster School of Business at the University of Washington in 2001 with a BA in international business, Japanese linguistics, and international economics. He loves traveling, languages, all things Star Wars (including collecting vintage boxed and graded Star Wars action figures), and anything from the 1980s. Blue has lived in the Seattle area for more than twenty years. He loves spending time with his wife Heidi and daughter Haiden and sharing his passions with them.

ABOUT BLUE STILEY'S LEADERSHIP & MENTORING COACHING

If you want to accelerate and improve your leadership skills, maximize your potential, gain the competitive advantage, grow or take your business success to the next level, ignite your passions, achieve your goals, strengthen you or your company's performance, and acquire the desire to do more tomorrow than you did today, then Blue Stiley's leadership and mentoring coaching is for you. Whether it is your work, business, health, finances, or relationships, his unique program will develop the guideposts to produce the winning formula required to achieve who you were meant to be in record time.

Don't feel overwhelmed because you don't know where to start or because you're not where you want to be. Let national and international self-leadership and life and business strategist Blue Stiley help you set your life vision, gain control of your life, become more confident, overcome fear and obstacles, improve health, and get the results you want by providing you with the necessary guidance and motivation to do what's necessary to realize those goals.

Whether it's through a one-on-one private or group coaching call, presentation, class, seminar, or workshop, Blue is one of the most talented mentors and coaches because he knows how to teach. He understands mentoring is about building trust, listening, making communication a two-way street, asking the right questions, being empathetic, and empowering others to become their best selves.

Blue has coached, mentored, and instructed thousands of people just like you, your team, or your business. He becomes your mentor to help guide you through all the steps in self-development and empowerment, to master all aspects of your personal and professional life, and to get you where you want to be.

For more information, visit one of the sites listed below, and then email Blue with your name, time zone, and the best time to reach you to redeem your no-obligation, self-development and mentoring consultation by phone or FaceTime.

www.BlueStiley.com
blue@bluestiley.com

BOOK BLUE STILEY TO SPEAK AT YOUR NEXT EVENT

When it comes to choosing a professional keynote speaker for your next event, Blue Stiley delivers actionable, motivational, and inspiring keynotes to maximize tangible results and peak performance through engaging stories and audience interaction. His powerful stage presence, knowledge, useful techniques, and fun and entertaining lessons will push attendees to completely transform their lives and renew their passions.

By speaking from experience, Blue instantly connects with attendees. He's an inspirational and natural storyteller, and his keynotes and events are full of real-life stories, powerful leadership strategies, anecdotes, takeaways, and actionable tools to take you or your business to the next level.

Every talk, speech, conference, seminar, event, and workshop Blue Stiley delivers is customized to maximize its relevance to your event's agenda. He always takes time to network and interview key stakeholders, clients, team members, and individuals to answer questions, meet specific requests, and review materials.

Whether your audience is ten or ten thousand, in North America or abroad, Blue Stiley's talks, book, and seminars are uplifting and highly engaging. He's humorous, inspirational, entertaining, extremely interactive, and provides proven strategies to change lives, accomplish goals, achieve extraordinary results, and create the best version of ourselves, personally and professionally, in a rapidly changing and competitive world.

If you're looking for a memorable speaker who will leave your audience wanting more, take action now and book Blue Stiley today! To see a highlight video of Blue Stiley and confirm him for your next meeting, visit his website or contact him by phone or email to schedule a complimentary pre-speech phone interview:

www.BlueStiley.com
blue@bluestiley.com